Resource organization in primary schools

Resource organization in primary schools

Second edition

Cecilia Gordon

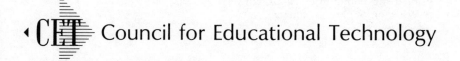

Council for Educational Technology

12461

Published by the Council for Educational Technology
3 Devonshire Street, London W1N 2BA

© Council for Educational Technology 1986

British Library Cataloguing in Publication Data

Gordon, Cecilia
    Resource organization in primary schools.
    — 2nd ed. — (Guidelines (Council for Educational Technology for the
    United Kingdom)), ISSN 0308-0323;5)
    1. Instructional materials centres — Administration
    I. Title   II. Council for Educational Technology for the United
    Kingdom   III. Series
    372.13'07'8   LB3044

    ISBN 0-86184-164-6

First published 1977
Reprinted 1978
Second edition 1986
ISBN 0 86184-164-6
ISSN 0308-0323

Typeset by H Charlesworth & Co Ltd
Deighton Road, Huddersfield HD2 1JJ

Printed and bound in Great Britain by
A Wheaton & Co Ltd, Exeter

Contents

Author's note to revised edition

Both editions of this book are very far from being 'all my own work'. The many people I have consulted have invariably been helpful and unbelievably generous with their time and effort. I cannot list them all but hope that I expressed my appreciation adequately on each occasion. I must, therefore, ask these kind people to accept this blanket acknowledgement and remember that, without them, this book could not have been written.

Cecilia Gordon
April 1986

Introduction

In librarians' jargon a school library is a 'special' library, which by definition means that it caters for a clientele whose members are identified by their distinctive needs. However, the whole clientele is by no means so clearly defined as that of, say, a library in a paint factory, whose demands are confined to one particular subject area. The users of a primary school library require coverage of a wide range of subject areas and consist of young children with specific, but often unpredictable, requests and also adults making sophisticated specialist demands to support their teaching.

The second edition of this book has been revised and updated to take account of the increasing availability of microcomputers and software. Its scope has, however, been deliberately limited to the brief implied by the title. 'Organization' implies procedures and we are forced to recognize that, in a primary school today, there is likely to be limited time, limited money and only basic library expertise. As far as possible, the very real temptation to enlarge on the exploitation of resources, especially electronic ones, has been avoided. The prospects are fascinating and exciting but discussion of these belongs to a different kind of book.

All materials in a primary library/resource centre must be both appropriate and accessible; achieving these criteria is the crux of the matter. It can and should be done, even for very young children, within the framework of conventional library organization, since the framework is flexible enough to allow endless adaptations and variations. From a very early stage, a child can be shown broad subject groupings and led on from this to an awareness of relationships and a skill in information retrieval that will later enable him to see the library as a relevant educational tool throughout his life.

To return to the two vital ingredients: appropriateness and accessibility. Appropriateness means including not only materials appropriate to the age and ability of the pupils, but also items intended specifically for use and interpretation by the teacher. Accessibility demands a retrieval system sophisticated enough to enable pupils to locate material for personally conceived topics, whose subject contents may cut right across the divisions of a conventional library classification system.

School library users — teachers and pupils alike — do not think like librarians. The former look for materials relevant to a concept or in a learning context; the latter sort materials, be they books or software, in accordance with their subject content. A library resource centre must be designed to respect both these attitudes and cope with widely divergent demands. The information retrieval system must be simple enough to be understood by users of varying age and ability and certainly not based on some mysterious formula devised by the coordinator.

Problems of this kind are deftly dealt with by a microcomputer. It may be as important these days for a child to learn how to use a computer as it has always been to learn to read; but the two skills are not mutually exclusive. Some basic literacy and numeracy are needed to understand and use a microcomputer and to profit from its suggestions. The technological explosion should not blind any- one to the intrinsic importance of reading for both information and delight. Whilst recognizing the growth of the microchip society, we have to accept that, for most primary schools, the gate to the promised land is not yet open. Realizing this, we have kept most of the DIY suggestions in the original text. There are many ingen- ious ideas to be recommended which are still relevant to the actual situation in an average school.

Provided we never forget that the subject content is more important than the medium, problems of classification and information retrieval are not too daunting. Problems of selection and storage, however, are new and tend to deter and confuse.

Most people have rudimentary ideas at least about book selection, and in subject areas the specialists' opinions can be respected. Libraries have always included books bought by special request, school libraries more than most. This practice, plus some overall coordination to ensure general coverage, has worked all right so far. But now that books have been supplemented by many other types of software we have a choice based not only on subject knowledge but also on preference for a particular medium. This may adversely affect the general usefulness of items bought since it may lead to cart-before-horse situations when software is chosen less for its suitability than to ensure that expensive machinery, perhaps rashly bought, will be utilized because it is there and needs justifying.

Sources for reviews of audio-visual material are multiplying, but the fact remains that it is even more vital to look at, or listen to, software before it is bought than it is to examine books. Parts of the country are well served in this respect: there are centres where teachers can assess both software and hardware and so make considered choices — if only they can find the time to go there. Other areas are desperately in need of such a service.

Ingenuity will go a long way towards solving the other problem — storage. Books are large or small, thin or thick, but conventional shelving is normally adaptable to all types. Now we are confronted by media of all shapes and sizes and must find logical, convenient ways of storing them. Expensive mistakes can be made, and it is only too easy to be lured by the wide selection of commercially produced storage units which are not necessarily compatible with a particular school's plans for the use of resources. Many primary schools depend to a large extent on do-it-yourself, and are the better for it. An astonishing variety of containers can be adapted for school use in much the same way as the infant teacher has always used toilet roll cores, egg boxes, moulds, yoghurt cartons, etc.

Support services to school libraries in the United Kingdom vary widely. Some schools receive practical advice and help from their authority, plus a centralized purchase system from which they receive their materials already classified and catalogued. At the other extreme there are individual schools which have evolved a system based solely on common sense and the recognized needs of staff and pupils. It is in the last area that some really ingenious ideas have been found; some, it must be confessed, are calculated to give a professional librarian the shudders (and a few are as ineffective in practice as they are unsound in theory) but most are nevertheless workable in a particular situation.

Demands for material for curriculum support multiply as the potential of a primary school library/resource centre becomes appreciated. However, much of the organization of most primary school centres is dictated by the accommodation available and by the amount of time the organizer can give to the centres. These two factors appear to be more important than finance. People other than teachers are of necessity involved — parents, ancillary helpers and children. It would not be appropriate in such circumstances to apply rigid professional conventions, or try to enforce elaborate procedures needing complicated descriptions and training.

This book attempts to isolate problems that are emerging in primary library/resource centre organization, and to record solutions that have been devised. To try to standardize procedures would be as unrealistic as to recommend positively particular solutions. The answer for one school might well be unhelpful for another. By looking squarely at problems and recording useful, practical ideas, it is hoped to encourage schools to develop their libraries into resource centres. Those who are already firmly committed to resource-based learning may find suggestions which will help them untangle at least some of the snags that have arisen.

This publication does not set out to examine case histories, but rather to present a distillation of findings and observations which, it is hoped, will be helpful to schools.

Attitudes, roles and users

It is becoming a truism to point out that fundamentally there is nothing new about resource-based learning. Suffice it to say here that the shock waves of the so-called explosion of educational technology have hit the secondary school harder than the primary one. Since teaching began, teachers have used what we now call 'resources', but this has always tended to be more generally and obviously true of primary teachers. Infant and junior school teachers have for many years been easily recognizable on public transport as they struggle with 'media': twigs and nests, seaweed and shells, plus rolls of pictures or charts, (ie printed visual aids).

The area where change has come about very rapidly is that defined by the need for machines. Even individualized working assignments based on handwritten workcards now demand a quick, efficient duplicating service. Many and varied copiers are now available, no need any more to stand for hours turning a handle. As for the electronic devices for sight and sound, they are increasingly available, domesticated and surprisingly cheap.

Thus many homes are now resource centres for recreation and information, with television, video and sophisticated audio systems. Nearly one in ten British households had a home computer in 1984 (Social Trends 16. 1986. HMSO). So it is not only teachers who have learnt to use microcomputers and associated equipment.

Children are quick to adapt to technology and are less daunted by buttons and knobs than many adults. Less able readers find it easier to start, stop and rewind a cassette recording than to find a place in a book. The possibility of improving reading by linking this facility with a text is obvious.

Also, the kind of participation (and progression) involved in using Language Masters, and later recording and playing back stories, can provide novelty, appeal and fresh motivation. Boredom, especially for the less able, is almost inevitable once a child becomes a passive listener or viewer, especially if the teacher withdraws too far or too often from the relationship. A disturbed, unhappy child needs a human being, not a machine. Television still holds considerable attraction for some children, but for others, it is only moving wallpaper that distracts their parents, or is used to distract them. Like other audio-visual aids, its effectiveness as a teaching aid can be greatly increased by teacher participation. A teacher working in a well-run, well-understood resource centre understands how to exploit its facilities to suit individual pupils, and the pupils have a choice of activity as well as some involvement in its management.

Primary schools committed to resource-based learning, whether based on a centralized resource area or operative throughout the teaching areas, do not need to be convinced of the concept, but often do need help with the organization, starting with the coordination of all the resources in the school.

The reason for referring to such teaching matters is that the growth of resource-based learning, and the consequent library resource centres, can now be seen to be changing the teacher's role. He can no longer be solely a disseminator of knowledge, but must to a larger extent also be a manager of resources. To support him in this role he needs to know not only their relevance to his subject, but also their suitability to his own attitudes, teaching techniques, aspects never dreamt of by those whose teaching remains based on chalk, talk and book. In addition, he needs to know what materials already exist in the school, what can be purchased to supplement this stock, what can be borrowed, and what can be produced tailor-made for his needs. Answering these questions is only an extension of the service an organized library, or a good school library service, will have been providing for years.

14

Opening up a collection of multi-media materials means that a teacher becomes a guide, training pupils to retrieve and effectively use all resources. Once trained, the pupils may well not pursue the line of inquiry the teacher expected. Such a situation of independence and interdependence may not be acceptable to all teachers. In addition, in these days of radio and television, the teacher is not necessarily in control of the subject content of the material that is being presented.

The attitude of a teacher to any kind of resource centre will be conditioned by how useful he finds it in his teaching. Some teachers may already have in their own teaching areas what amount to satellite resource centres and may well be unwilling to share carefully hoarded materials, quite unmoved by the argument that lending also implies the right to borrow. Some regard the whole concept of centralization of resources with suspicion and distrust.

So, from the attitude of individual teachers we come to the all important consensus of opinion in the school. Most primary teachers, though by no means all, are to some degree committed to resource-based learning. But how do they feel about exploring new ideas together and centralizing all resources? Such concepts can seem very threatening to teachers in conventional schools who teach behind closed classroom doors. And this despite the assurances of those in open-plan schools who are accustomed to the movement of groups and to team teaching. Centralization needs to be made acceptable as well as effective. It need not necessarily mean putting actual objects all together in one place, but it does demand listing items for everyone's convenience and, above all, sharing. In fact, the definition of centralization depends on many factors, including the age range of the children and the exigencies of the school building.

Even non-cooperation by a small minority can cause confusion and the entire enterprise can be made totally ineffective if staff are not entirely convinced of what is needed. A costly resource centre established to enforce change will most probably turn out to be a white elephant. In one extreme case, a headmaster insisted on having a resource centre and set it up at the end of a covered way on the edge of the school complex. As a result of his attitude and its position, the resource centre is grossly under-used and there appears to be very little communication between the 'resources assistant' and the teaching staff.

Other resource centres have evolved almost by chance as materials have accumulated until at some point it has dawned on everyone that the existing haphazard arrangement is wasteful and inefficient. *What* to do about it is a far less knotty problem than who is to do it. Later we can consider staff quotas, hours available and local education authorities' attitudes, but the first consideration is personal relationships! In a primary school the appointment will be of a coordinator, teacher with post of responsibility, clerical officer or whatever. But whoever is appointed *must* be generally acceptable to the staff. Such a person needs to keep up continual rapport with the teachers and should take the initiative in consulting with both staff and pupils. To assume that they will spontaneously come forward with either suggestions or queries can lead to increasing isolation of the centre.

Any resentments about decisions are bound to inhibit communications and the sharing of both ideas and materials. So it is obvious that a great deal of discussion, consultation and investigation must go on before such a drastic change as centralizing resources can even be considered.

In general, it is unlikely that any head, or any minority group, can successfully impose an organization of resources without the willing cooperation of the majority of the staff. If the tone of enthusiasm and understanding of all the implications stem from the head, who is at the same time willing to listen to opposing points of view and consider personal misgivings, there will be little opposition to reorganization. Some teachers may not be interested at first. They have evolved their own ways of teaching and, like many another, are apprehensive of new ideas, of new alternatives to their hard-learned and tested methods. Others are not happy about handling electronic machinery, especially in a group situation.

Most of these will be converted once the library resource area (or the reorganization of resources) has proved its worth. They will see what an excellent support service it is to teachers and what a source of new ideas and approaches to curriculum development. They will find increased pupil interest and motivation.

However, a few diehards may remain detached and sceptical. But a tactful head and a tolerant staff will not allow them to distract others from the benefits of resource-based learning. Besides, one must accept that many experienced teachers continue to teach very well in the old-fashioned way! After all, in the final analysis it is personality that counts, in the classroom or anywhere else.

Discussions and decisions

At some stage an agreed decision must be taken about the actual physical arrangement of things. It is all very well listing items and agreeing to share them. But it is essential to know where they are!

There are numerous factors to consider before actually putting resources together and all must be discussed and considered if a sensible ongoing arrangement is to be evolved and at least the worst pitfalls avoided.

To start at the beginning, the degree of actual centralization is conditioned, among other factors, by the age and ability of the children. The best infant schools are in themselves resource centres and so, in a less obvious way, are junior schools committed to resource-based learning. The difference is rather one of degree, as juniors require slightly more detailed systems because their demands are more specific. An open-plan infant school will have such features as 'listening posts' and subject areas tucked away around the teaching and quiet areas. In a classroom-designed school, each room will have its mini-collection and some selection of media will be instantly available to pupils.

Whatever the physical features of a school, the arrangements must be flexible and simple enough to be understood by the children. It is easy to get too pretentious in discussing the organization of resources for infants. Whatever the 5-to-6 year old is doing —

talking while he plays, increasing his reading skill or listening to stories — he is developing language and all is grist to his mill. However, even for young children there needs to be basic organization of resources to meet simple demands. It is never too early to start the idea of relationships by grouping like to like by subject content. To do this, items need to be marked according to some code used consistently for all media. Colour coding based on broad subject divisions is easily understood and widely adaptable. For instance, an open-plan school will have permanent displays of books grouped by subject, such as 'living things'. The area will be characterized by a large coloured square on the wall and small matching coloured labels on the books. The relevant software may be stored elsewhere, but it will be colour coded too, so that it is a simple matter to match, say, a book on lions with slides or filmstrips.

In a classroom school, even at infant level, there is a valid argument for a particular kind of physical centralization, especially of books. A central stock will fill two needs; firstly it can help to keep classroom collections alive and interesting, and secondly can offer a back-up information service. Classroom collections, being of necessity small, can quickly become over-familiar. Bearing in mind that three months is a long time to a young child, it would seem a good idea to recall items to the main collection at the end of each term. This gives the coordinator a chance to check the condition of stock and keep it up to date. Next term, each teacher can borrow a fresh collection and so books, especially, are kept circulating. Such an arrangement also breaks down any tendency towards that possessive attitude which militates against sharing. Obviously, each classroom will have its own basic, permanent collection of information materials, plus dictionaries, atlases, etc, but everything else should circulate, especially story books.

Any hardware that is going to be loaned from a central store needs to be portable and readily available. Some schools, after trying this fetch-and-carry method, have had so much damage done by careless or ignorant handling of valuable equipment that they have been forced to apply rigid rules and allow only a very select few to collect hardware. Others run a booking system which is administered by an ancillary helper who consults the requests made by teachers and sets up what is required. Yet other schools train children as monitors who act in pairs and can be trained to be very adept in setting up or loading equipment. A school's decisions about hardware will depend on many things: frequency of use of this or that piece of equipment, positioning of storage areas (up or down stairs) and so on. A separate section on hardware discusses these factors in detail.

If a school comes finally to favour the centralization of resources, the next important question is where. Followed of course by how, but we come to that later. In areas where school rolls may be dropping, a classroom can often be freed to be converted to a library. Provided the room is large enough and well sited, this is a perfectly practical solution. Some old schools have been provided with new halls or gymnasia, leaving the old hall, usually in the centre of the building, vacant. Other single-decker schools were built round internal open courtyards which can be roofed over. Cloakroom areas are often well placed and can easily be adapted. In these days, the simplest, cheapest solution is likely to be the only option open. But whatever economies have to be made, the choice of position must be given absolute priority. A centralized library/resource centre should be nearer the younger children, and must never be down a chilly corridor or across a corner of the playground. It should be in fact, as well as in spirit, the hub of the school.

Having chosen an area, there will still be the problems of storage and shelving, of floor coverings and socket outlets. Let us leave these problems for the moment and consider whether the chosen area is suitable for the kind of adaptations that will make it different from a classroom because a library should look and feel different from a classroom.

This statement is in no way intended to denigrate classrooms, the matter is one of difference. It is not easy to describe exactly what this difference is, it is a combination of attitudes of people and the appearance of the room. Once achieved, everyone appreciates it and benefits from it.

19

Classrooms in primary schools are colourful places, full of interesting objects, displays and examples of children's work, as well as picture posters and nature tables. The children must feel that the library is an equally attractive place which they visit for their own purposes, to pursue their own interests and in which they feel relaxed. Children's sections in public libraries are far from being the dull corners they used to be and the school library has to compete with them. Many children's first contact with a library will be in school and will condition their life-long attitude to libraries. Conversely, others may be taken by parents to their local library and will make invidious comparisons if their school library is neglected or untidy.

Curtains and carpets are important assets to a library. They create a warm, welcoming atmosphere and also deaden sound. It is not reasonable to expect total silence in a library, children need to ask questions and should not be discouraged from quietly discussing matters that interest them. But the noise must be kept to an absolute minimum, if only for the sake of those who want to read or listen on their own.

Storage furniture should be attractive and practical, providing, if possible, extra work surfaces. The shelving should be attractively arranged, avoiding a regimented look. A visual subject index, simple charts or clear notices, explaining colour coding or classification, diagrams or simple flow charts showing 'how to find out' — these are all things that create the impression that the library is offering something personal and special to each child.

Constantly varied displays of special books, or other material of topical interest, will alert young readers to new ideas. Children should be encouraged (but not obliged) to write their own book reviews. These need not be literary masterpieces, but if they are pinned up in the library, others will be encouraged to read something they know a contemporary has enjoyed.

The whole concept of children coming to a library and using it as a support to their classroom work does not necessarily imply total centralization. They can of course visit special areas for specific information, but it must be remembered that the more completely centralized the resources, the more availability depends on organization and supervision. It is possible to find an immaculate library/resource centre where the door is locked for most of the day, and others where classes are rigidly timetabled and spontaneous use of the resources is discouraged. If centralizing your resources is going drastically to reduce their availability, think again.

Availability at all times is easiest to achieve in open-plan schools where there can be complete freedom of movement without disturbing others. All materials can be dispersed to strategic areas throughout the school in subject corners or whatever. Clearly, this implies carefully kept records and stocklists, and some control of borrowing.

If conditions in your school and the attitudes of your colleagues have convinced you that the time has come to centralize your resources, the next section makes some practical suggestions to help you.

If, on the other hand, you decide that centralization is not for you, suggestions about organization of and retrieval systems for dispersed collections will be found in a later section.

Planning your centre

The major part of this section will assume that you are faced with
the task of adapting existing conditions to suit your decision to
have a centralized library/resource area. 'Adaptation' may well
involve considerable alterations and be quite costly. You will do
well to be familiar with local regulations for minor building works.
There have always been limitations on spending, and arguments
about who should pay for what, and the economic climate may
not be encouraging for rebuilding or demolition, regardless of how
valuable the change may be. Adaptations which do not involve any
structural alterations, such as moving shelving or providing carpets
and curtains, are more easily negotiated and much less expensive.
It is to be hoped that the people most closely involved in operating
the resource centre will be consulted at every step in the planning
of changes.

New buildings
The head and staff should be consulted at the earliest stage in the
planning of a new primary school and must continue to be involved as the work proceeds. Other books go into such things as
building recommendations in some detail, so it is pointless to go
over the same ground here. (See *The Design of Learning Spaces*
by Peter Smith, CET 1974 and *Adapting Spaces for Resource-Based
Learning* by Barbara Atherton, CET 1980.)

As for the vital matter of consultation, it is all a matter of timing
and insisting on seeing architects' plans before the building is
started and it is too late to alter anything. There have been various
Department of Education and Science pronouncements and

23

building bulletins laying down standards for primary school libraries. These mostly fall short of the recommendations of the Library Association and other interested groups. As long ago as 1888, the Cross Commission Report said that 'the establishment of school libraries is strongly to be recommended' and this has been echoed by numerous reports since, from Cross to Bullock and beyond.

In late 1984 came 'School Libraries: the foundations of the curriculum', a detailed report of the Library and Information Services Council's (LISC) working party on school library services. Although it is predominantly relevant to secondary schools, and more concerned with policy than planning, every primary school teacher/librarian should be aware of its recommendations and strictures.

However, the sad truth is that, in the present era of educational cuts, plans for new primary schools are being submitted without provision for a central collection. Even the alternative, providing areas for a dispersed collection, is not adequately considered. Shelving is suggested in 'quiet' areas, plus so-called 'library' areas, which are often only alcoves adjoining practical areas or halls. This is a retrograde step from the 1950s when some authorities began to include in their plans for new schools space for having a central collection. Indeed, today, people in older schools are sometimes better off regarding library accommodation because many of them actually have a separate room designated 'the library'.

However, should plans for a new school include a purpose-built library, there are things you may be able to control in ways not possible for those adapting existing conditions. These include heating and lighting. The heating system should not take up wall space needed for shelving, and the desire for natural lighting should not result in a glass-sided room with perhaps only one solid wall suitable for shelving. Strip lighting casts fewer shadows and is more economical than separate hanging lights. Other points to note are, of course, the siting of the room and the position of the exit in relation to the movement of pupils.

Starting from where you are

Obviously, when contemplating any drastic move, or reorganization of resources, there are general considerations to be thought of, no matter what the present conditions are. Some heating systems seem to demand a proliferation of pipes, others manage with a couple of radiators neatly stowed away. A room lined with pipes and radiators is difficult to adapt to library use — you cannot shelve books above hot radiators; and remember that tapes must be kept cool and stored away from anything electro-magnetic (loudspeakers, transformers, etc).

Free-standing shelf units are one answer to restricted wall areas for shelving but they do reduce the space available for chairs and tables and constrict the free movement of children — or encourage the wrong type of movement.

Look at your chosen room bearing in mind how you intend to use it. As far as possible everyone must be agreed about this, if only to avoid future arguments. A wide variety of uses must be considered as it is likely that individual ideas and intentions will vary considerably.

Basic possible uses can be narrowed down to a list from which to start discussion. Some possibilities are:

class visits
individual study (topic research and writing)
individual quiet reading
individual viewing
small group viewing
occasions for browsing and choosing books and other media.

These possibilities all have to be considered in the context of the library organization and staffing, as well as the physical characteristics and limitations of the room.

A large proportion of the stock will probably be kept on wall shelving but free-standing (or island) units are flexible if the room needs rearranging, provided they are not so high as to obscure vision for supervision. Not all walls are strong enough to take wall

25

shelving. But some makers have designed wall shelving which is only secured to the wall, the actual weight being taken by the floor.

Some walls may be painted white and used as a backing to working surfaces, for individual viewing or displays. Opaque screens can be used in the same way and have the added advantage of being easily moved to create small areas temporarily reserved for one pupil or a small group.

The placing of electric plugs in relation to working surfaces and to shelving must be carefully considered. Do not put a socket in a wall and later decide you would rather have had shelving there. In a converted classroom there may be a sink which will make one area totally unsuitable for the use of audio-visual resources, since no electrical device must be used near water.

In the list of activities what is often called 'teachers' preparation' has deliberately been omitted. Some secondary schools are aiming to include 'teacher preparation rooms' in the library/resource centres. Facilities here usually include provision for making teaching/learning resources and reprographic services. In primary school it is more sensible to align these activities with the school office. Hopefully this will be close to the library, and the equipment will be available when required without impeding work of the office staff.

Other separations, less rational, may be forced on you because of lack of space. You may find it expedient to separate books from other media, or fiction books from information retrieval areas.

On the other hand, you may be lucky enough to have space to include everything under one ceiling. It is not proposed here to go into details about recommended areas for different activities or storage. Such things are well dealt with in the professional literature (see bibliography) and each school will have to consider its own situation.

The Library Association has made positive recommendations on space requirements in relation to the size of the school and suggests proportional allocation of areas for different purposes. The section on furnishing library areas in primary schools is particularly helpful and gives simple rules of thumb to be applied. For example, a shelf a metre long will hold 40 books shelved spines outwards, but many books in primary schools will be displayed front cover outwards. In these display areas, a metre shelf will only take about 5 books. A stock of 8 books per child is recommended, and how the books are arranged must depend on how the centre is used. All schools face the problem of having to provide storage for books in holidays. This is a problem not faced by public libraries who reckon to have one-third of their stock out on loan all the time.

It is very difficult to lay down similar guidelines in estimating how much space will be needed for audio-visual materials. This depends on how it is stored, as much as on quantity. Some media (eg cassettes and packs) can be stored on shelving, others (eg filmstrips, slides, overhead projector transparencies and charts) need special provision. This is examined in detail in the section on storage. It is safe to say that one should allow as much space as possible – once established a centre will expand rapidly.

To try to put all the arguments into a helpful context, even at the risk of over-simplification, we can divide schools planning basic reorganization of resources into three categories. Even if your school does not exactly fit into one of these categories it is hoped you will find some suggestions useful to you.

In each situation, the possibility of help, financial, practical or professional, from parents must not be overlooked. A parent-teacher association function to raise money for a specific enterprise or purchase is usually successful and several schools mention generous gifts in kind from managers and parents. Practical help is a bit more tricky. Simple carpentry is no problem, but obviously such things as electric wiring or drastic alterations can only be done with the authority's approval and by qualified people.

A school with scattered resources
This school feels the time has come for actual centralization and is looking for a focal point.

Some suggestions as to the kind of areas to look at have already been made. Let us look at each possibility specifically, not forgetting the general principles involved.

A classroom

Firstly, a vacant classroom. The amount of shelving possible will be dictated partly by the wall space available — low windows may break up the outside wall, but high windows need not interfere with shelving which should not be more than 3ft high in infant schools or 4ft in junior schools. The partition wall with the corridor may be only wood panels with glass above and the remaining wall may include a chimney buttress! Instead of wall areas, island shelving may be used, but it must not be too high and must be arranged so that no part of the library is hidden from sight. This does not rule out using shelving to create quiet reading areas. As always, consideration must be given to separating noisy, fussy activities from quiet ones.

Furniture for storage for software must not be forgotten when considering room arrangement. Many storage units are low and can double as room dividers and working surfaces.

A cloakroom

Secondly, cloakroom areas of the kind often seen in old schools are very adaptable. Two diagrams here are based on conversions successfully made. In one case, two adjacent connecting cloakroom areas were carpeted with industrial carpet tiles and fitted with shelving.

Pegs were transferred to battens on an adjacent wall in the corridor. Figure 1A shows how this could be done with a single cloakroom bay. Nearby in the entrance hall, in an area which had formerly contained books in glass-fronted bookcases, benches and power points were fixed to make a working area.

In another school (Figure 1B) the old fashioned cloakroom unit was left as a room divider. Pegs were removed inside the library area but retained outside for continued use. The bench in the unit was retained in the library as there was not room for any other seating.

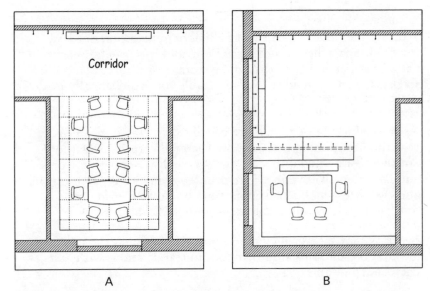

A   B

Figure 1. Plans showing how cloakrooms may be converted into library/resource areas

Above the bench are displays of work, etc, while the two structural walls are fitted with shelving. This conversion provided the school with a much-improved book library, but audio-visual material had to be kept and used elsewhere.

The disadvantage of cloakroom adaptation is that there will be no door, so supervision during the school day and security outside school hours can be a problem. One school overcame this by putting up white painted metal fencing with a lockable gate. The effect is most attractive and does not exclude light or air (which can be a problem in small rooms) even when closed. If the cloakroom area is on the ground floor, there should be no fire risk but the situation shown in Figure 1B is in a junior school on the first floor and the whole question of exits and fire risks had to be carefully considered.

The shape of a cloakroom can be turned to an advantage because it may be easier to create quiet areas and make some separation of activities than it would be to do so in a plain square classroom.

A hall
Thirdly, the possibility of using a hall or gymnasium not now required. Space here is not a problem, and it is usual to partition parts of the area. Partitions can be storage furniture, island book stacks, screens (provided they are stable) or professionally made partitions.

As the ceilings in such halls are usually very high it is not likely that the partitioning will do more than indicate areas, without cutting off noise, and this can be a grave disadvantage. Carpets and hessian wall coverings (fire-proofed) can cut down resonance, and the latter can be backed by fibre board to provide good display mounting and a colourful pleasant ambience.

Security may be a problem but there should be no fire risk as such, as these rooms are usually in central positions with exits at each end.

An entrance hall, or ground-floor corridor, is worth considering for a book collection. It is not very suitable for software which is less attractive visually when stored. A well arranged collection of books will be noticed at once by parents and other visitors, who will see it as obviously an important feature of the school.

A school with a large entrance hall, or lobby, can, by the imaginative use of screens or pegboard partitions plus a few chairs and carpets, create the right welcoming and interesting impression.

Many schools are driven by overcrowding to put up bookshelves in unsuitable corridors. Any corridor needs critical consideration. Long rows of books do not look very attractive and there are strict fire regulations which must be observed. In addition to the consideration of fire hazards, wide clearance is needed so that children can safely use the corridor as a passage, even when others are standing at the shelves. A corridor is a sensible place to have reference books that may be needed in a hurry by more than one class.

A courtyard
Finally, the idea of using a central courtyard. This, though attrac-

30

tive, may prove to be very expensive. It will have to be roofed over and floored under, provided with top lighting and planned from scratch, probably using only free-standing shelving. Advantages are that the area will be surrounded by windowed corridors into which all classrooms lead, so links with the resource centre are visible and real and the centre literally *is* the centre.

A school with a small book room
There is a lot to be said for retaining a small book room as a quiet reading area. One educational priority area school has a charming little book room in a converted cloakroom. There are curtains at the windows and carpets and big cushions on the floor. The area is used before and after school, for quiet reading and story telling as well as for changing books during the day. The school wanted a centralized resource centre but resisted the idea of disbanding the little book room, even though there was a room large enough to take all media. There is also a convent school in an old building which has a delightful room with bay windows looking on to the garden and this too has been retained as a book room, with a well developed library resource area down the corridor. The criteria for these separations were clear enough at the time, but there are snags. The epa school is an infant school so it is clear that the resource centre is for finding out and the book room for reading, but the other school is a junior school and the attempt to separate reading for pleasure from information retrieval is not wholly successful. Poetry, plays, myths and legends are out of place in the working atmosphere of one room and there is a wealth of information concealed in the fiction books.

Superficially, it does seem reasonable to protect quiet readers from the fussy fidgety business of information retrieval and from the distractions caused by setting up and using audio-visual material. As has already been said, this must be considered in planning. It is the degree of separation that matters. A room nearby on the same floor, or better still a room next door which can be connected with the present library, are reasonable compromises. If you are lucky enough to secure the room next door, a communicating door, or an archway, knocked through the party wall will unite the two rooms quite satisfactorily. What remains of the separating wall is an asset if it divides noisy activities from quiet contemplation. How much wall can be knocked down, and where, depends of course on which walls are load bearing, and nothing can be done without expert advice and consideration of the original building plan.

Never consider any amalgamation that ends up with more than one entrance (or exit) to your library/resource centre. If two rooms are connected together, the original entrance to one of them must be kept closed. If there is a fire risk, a key behind glass inside the door will be a wise precaution. These remarks of course do not apply to opening up a whole area already fairly accessible. One school achieved an excellent union between an open area for books and a room storing audio-visual aids. The shared wall was taken down to within a few feet of the ground and a working surface is fixed on this low room divider. So in this school, books and other media are united by what could have been a barrier. The child or teacher thinks of everything in terms of subject content, with choice of media a secondary consideration.

However, should the only other available room be a long way away from the book room, the drastic step of merging media should be seriously considered. Standard book shelving can be moved without undue labour (just carefully measure up beforehand). The whole concept of a library/resource centre is that the media are complementary. If two areas are widely separated, there is a danger that people will tend just to use the one nearest to them, thus depriving themselves of half the resources available.

The multi-purpose room
Sometimes one finds in a school a room which was once a library but which has gradually lost its identity. There are books there and children do come to browse, or look for information, but it has gradually become a dumping ground for musical instruments, games kit, costume, scenery, etc. Or it is regularly used for medicals, music lessons or rehearsals.

Changes of staff attitudes towards classroom libraries, or the loss of a coordinator, or long absence of a head, may have brought about

32

this situation. It may, however, be because the room is badly sited, at the very top of the building or at the end of a long corridor. If this is the case it is unwise to consider such a room as an area for centralizing resources.

However, if it is agreed that the room is suitable for a library/resource centre, two problems must first be resolved. Decisions must be taken as to where to store equipment, etc, unrelated to a library/resource centre, and where to timetable such activities as medicals, music lessons and rehearsals. Solving these problems is easier said than done. But taking over a library/resource centre for other activities, even if strictly timetabled, cuts down drastically on its services to the school and miscellaneous storage must *not* be allowed. There is, however, no reason why small remedial groups should not continue to use the room.

If you have solved these problems, start to build up your library/ resource centre on the book stock already there. First weed out ruthlessly all shabby and out-of-date books. Then consider the shelving: is it varied, should you have more free-standing units or display stands?

Consider the whole room in terms of multi-media storage and use. Probably there will be no need for structural alterations but the room should be divided into defined areas. This can be done either by screens or by the imaginative arrangement of furniture and storage units. Low storage units provide work tops and are sometimes more effective room dividers than screens. Pinboard screens make display areas, but they do block the light. Wire mesh screens look very effective, do not block the light and can be used for displays of selected new books. Plants too can be hung on the plastic hooks provided.

Other points have been mentioned in other sections. Check them in relation to your room.

It will be some time before such a room settles down. Do not make any irrevocable decisions until you are sure they fit in with the use of the room as it develops. The only thing that should be, so to speak, screwed down, is the shelving. Everything else should be movable so that the basic arrangement is flexible. However carefully the plans have been discussed things will emerge in use that were never envisaged. Uses of the room will develop in unexpected ways and planning will be a continuous process in relation to how the pupils and teachers come to use the resources and what demands are made to match curriculum changes.

Open up your cupboards
After open minds come open cupboards or, in more formal terms, 'coordinating existing resources in the school'. This must be done before embarking on any major reorganization or contemplating major expenditure on stock from a planned resource centre.

Great quantities of forgotten material will be found tucked away in odd corners or behind closed cupboard doors. Some of it will be out of date, but most of it will be extremely useful and there are sure to be some items of equipment only needing minor repairs but unused because no one organized their salvation.

The passing of time will actually have rendered some materials more valuable. Photographs of past events, postcards, local history material and magazines recording events are examples of maturing material. Old maps, geography books, faded charts and out-of-date equipment are examples of decaying material!

Although the tact, persistence and physical effort involved in coordinating cannot be minimized, it does pay a handsome dividend. Many a school has said 'we have not really got much in the way of resources' only to find throughout the building disorganized collections of materials perfectly suited to be rearranged in a resources centre.

Fortunately this task is a once-for-all job. Once materials are centrally recorded you have a basis on which to build a library/ resource centre even if the things themselves are still scattered around. It may not be possible to call in materials; there may be nowhere to put them. It will cause less inconvenience and no disruption of use to leave them where they are for the time being,

34

unless it is clear that they are not being used in which case they need reassessing or re-allocation.

Probably the best plan is to ask each teacher to go through cupboards and stock room and selectively list all items of audiovisual material (both hardware and software). Such lists can then be collated by the coordinator or, better still, by a small working party of teachers, who can then review the situation and consider the next step. Coordinating hardware needs a different approach from coordinating software, so there is a separate section on hardware organization.

The basis of a library/resource centre must be an organized collection of books properly classified, and at some early stage the books must be examined and if necessary weeded out quite ruthlessly and checked for gaps in subject coverage. Out-of-date books are a waste of space in a school library which should be seen as a working tool, not a store house. Discarding of fiction should depend more on the condition of the book than upon its date of publication. Many children read avidly stories enjoyed by their grandparents.

Before disposing of information books check for pictures which might be useful pasted on to workcards, or used as expendable material by pupils or teachers. The contents of scientific or technical books will need selection, whereas most of the pictures in nature study or history books will be useful.

This is the time to look at the book organization and decide whether the present system can accommodate other media. If your book collection has been organized simply within the framework of conventional library practice this should be no problem. If you have a subject index, a subject or classified catalogue, an author catalogue and clear notices and shelf guides, incorporating software presents only problems of storage. If you have only a subject index and your book records are only stock records it is still a matter of adapting to one new factor. Your inquirer needs to be told the physical form of an item he has traced in the records which relate to his subject.

Should it become obvious that the present organization of books is too vague, too idiosyncratic or too inflexible to take the strain of including and describing other kinds of software, it must be changed. The organization of books has been carefully considered for many years now and books are still, in many ways, the most compact and flexible medium of knowledge. So it is certainly reasonable to base the organization of a multi-media collection on a tried and tested practice based on the subject content of books.

The cataloguing (ie listing and describing of each item) of materials may well reveal duplications which are a waste of money. In future this can be avoided by simply checking a list or index to see whether the item it is proposed to buy is already in the school.

Classification (ie arranging of items and the description of items in subject groups) will reveal gaps in subject coverage which can now be considered and remedied. The objects themselves will be labelled to match the colours or symbols for subject content used in the list or card index. This use of symbols is explained in detail in another section. Once the library/resource centre is organized, items are best arranged by subject content, even if the media are separated, each having its own subject sequence.

The other information needed is where the item is located. This will only be an interim problem if you are intending eventually to centralize resources. But meanwhile on every card in an index, and on every list distributed to teachers, there must be an indication of where to go and find what is wanted.

At the central point of organization card indexes are preferable to lists which quickly become messy and out of date. One can quickly compile a list from a card index and conversely the items on a list can easily be added to a card index. It is therefore suggested that from the lists submitted by teachers of their holdings a master index on 5in × 3in cards arranged in subject order be compiled. A card index is flexible, it can be added to and subtracted from with no difficulty.

The filing must be done only by someone who clearly understands the principles involved in the sequence. Cards should never be removed for any reason (except permanently to alter the record) and care must be taken not to tilt the container, unless the cards are secured by a rod.

This is an area in which a microcomputer can be of immense benefit. If you have easy access to one, it can be used to provide a system that is easy to control, flexible, and quick and simple to update.

For some time, while you are coordinating your resources and perhaps moving towards complete centralization, your methods of organization will be much the same as those in a school which has decided on dispersed resources. You must keep your teachers informed of what is available in other parts of the school and of new additions to stock. Solutions to this and other coordination–communication problems are discussed in the section 'organizing dispersed resources' so they will not be repeated here. Read the two sections as complementary.

Organizing dispersed resources
There are many reasons why dispersed resources, or satellite resource centres, may be better for your school than the kind of centralized arrangements that have been discussed so far. There may be absolutely nowhere in the school that could be adapted for a library/resource centre or teachers may be positively against centralizing resources. They may prefer resource areas with all kinds of teaching and learning materials in each year area, or in subject-based satellite centres. There are good arguments for having immediately to hand materials you want to use or for having them already sorted for topic work. Infant schools are often excellent examples of how well organized dispersed collections can be. It is pretentious nonsense to talk too much about centralized resources and complicated retrieval methods for little children, for whom everything should be freely available when they want it. However, there does need to be some uniformity of arrangement, and some centralized organization, or materials will be either under-used and forgotten, or money will be wasted on duplication.

Books and materials need to be arranged in an agreed system of colour coding or Dewey numbering, which implies a central record of stock and someone in charge of processing new materials as they arrive. This will not be easy to do if teachers are allocated money to spend as they wish, but even a simple accessions register with location symbols would help to coordinate materials. Some method must be devised for stock taking and such a central record can be used for this. It really is very useful to have a central catalogue of all the resources in the school. This should consist of simple descriptions of items and where they can be found and should be available to be consulted by all the teachers. Without this it is hard to see how any sharing of materials can be organized.

If it is agreed that teachers are prepared to lend materials a careful record of loans must be kept by the lender.

Classrooms, or resource areas, should have visible subject indexes, no matter how small the collection, so that the children are getting some training in information retrieval and will learn to apply the

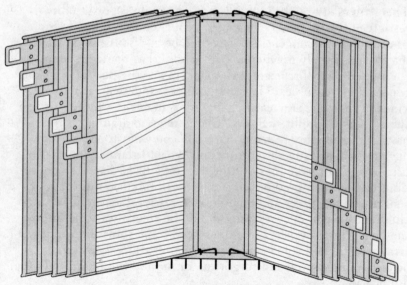

Figure 2. Strip index mounted on wall to provide visible subject index

skills learnt to finding materials outside their own area. This should be flexible enough to adjust to regular changes of material.

Stripdex panels mounted at child's eye height on wall brackets can provide a visible subject index that 'can be turned like a book'. These can have several forms and be used as individual class indexes as well as for the centralized index. Provided that light coloured strips are used, and the cellophane protective sheets removed beforehand, these can be copied on an electrostatic copier to provide an easily updated union catalogue, one per class. A year later fresh copies can be made from updated panels. The strips can be arranged in any preferred way, to make a subject index or a catalogue of actual items. They can include class numbers, location and indication of media. Strips of another colour can be used to indicate non-book media.

It is possible to make one's own wall mounts using 1in angle strips of the sort for making edgings to kitchen furniture.

One danger inherent in satellite centres is that books especially can be left in the rooms year after year, the argument being that a new set of children arrives at the beginning of each year and to them this will be a fresh collection of books. But before long 'fresh' is hardly an apt word. One head, quite committed to dispersed collections, did actually confess that the books 'do become a bit tatty'. In a school with vertically grouped classes a child can be in the same teaching area for a considerable time and is not going to be encouraged to read a book he has seen around month after month, even if by now he has achieved the age and ability to read and enjoy it.

Another disadvantage is that the children's choice is limited to the materials available in their area or classroom. Something must be done, especially with the books, to keep the stock fluid. Borrowing collections from the schools library service or public library and changing them every term is one way of doing this. Another way is to have a central collection, in a stock room perhaps, which is used as a pool from which books are regularly borrowed and returned. Sharing and discussion should be encouraged, to avoid the situation described by one librarian, who visits schools in a mobile library van. She reported that sometimes one teacher will select what another has just returned. Which certainly seems to indicate the need for planning and coordination within the school!

The situation however may not have been quite as crazy as the librarian imagined. Very likely each teacher borrowed her own collection and jealously guarded it for her own use. In any case one would not recommend topic material, or individually chosen collections, *borrowed* from outside sources being integrated into the school stock. This makes retrieval of the books, when they are due back, a time-consuming, irritating problem.

No one should run away with the idea that a well organized centralized resource centre, freely available to all, precludes the idea of classroom collections. In 1958 the School Library Association came out with this firm statement about classroom libraries:

'Classroom libraries, therefore, must not be thought of as an inferior and cheaper makeshift and as a mere substitute for the library in a secondary school. They are the ideal form of library for children of primary school age, they offer immense opportunities to the teacher; and every school can make a start in establishing them straight away'.

Nearly thirty years later, one cannot disagree with the statement, provided the classroom library is constantly refreshed and consists of rather more than a basic reference collection. Bullock 21.6 suggests 'an encyclopedia, a good dictionary, a good atlas, a collection of books varying across the children's interests and touching all the major areas of the curriculum, a shelf of poetry and a range of fiction'. Both SLA and Bullock recognize that books lose their attraction for children if they remain unchanged for too long.

Even if books are arranged within reach all over the classroom, there should also be a partly enclosed corner in the quietest part of the room with large cushions and a piece of carpet to make a welcome retreat, as well as offer encouragement to private reading.

There are so many factors for and against centralization, one can only sum up by quoting Bullock again; 'The important thing is that there should be a clear and recognized system of organization which allows everyone to know what are the school's resources and how they are dispersed'.

Organization and use of materials

Definitions
Two terms, 'hardware' and 'software', are bandied about freely
amongst librarians and teachers, but not all of them are clear what
they mean and some would give different definitions from others.
The use of the term 'non-book materials' adds to the confusion.

To start from the premise that all software needs a machine before
it can be used seems safe enough. Until one comes across people
who refer to charts, pictures, workcards, pamphlets and cuttings
as 'software'.

For practical purposes one has to have a code to warn an inquirer
who has found, in the catalogue, an item relevant to his topic, that
it cannot be used without a piece of equipment. So we devise
colour coding to designate media or simply use a different coloured
card for anything that is not printed material and needs a piece of
equipment. We also explain what it is by writing 'filmstrip', etc,
beside the Dewey number, or using some code. But there still remains the problem of distinguishing a mass of printed material
which is not in book form. We find this described as 'non-book
print material' or by some other awkward phrase.

In this publication 'software' means any item that is symbiotic
with a machine, useless without it.

Hardware
This section will deal separately with the rationalization, use
and storage of mechanical teaching aids — ie, of such items of

equipment as overhead projectors, slide viewers, TV sets, micro-computers and visual display units (VDUs) — and will refer to them all as 'hardware'.

Hardware in a school is really the back-up service to the whole concept of resource-based learning, so its use, maintenance and storage are very important. Each item of audio-visual equipment has its own physical characteristics which largely determine how it is stored, maintained and under what conditions it needs to be used.

Selection, supply and purchase
Conditions of supply and regulations about purchase of hardware vary from one local education authority to another. How your hardware is bought and supplied will affect the relevance of the rest of this section to your school. If your local authority equips you with a standard 'package' of equipment and runs an efficient, quick maintenance service some points raised here will not apply to you. But not everyone is so fortunate.

It really is worth making an exhaustive check of your hardware and equally important to consider carefully before equipment is bought. Suggestions made in this section are intended to apply both to a school assessing and reorganizing existing stocks of hardware and also to one considering buying hardware and turning increasingly to resource-based learning.

Here are some points to consider before deciding whether to retain a machine, or before buying one.

Is the item up to date or has something reasonably cheap and better superseded it?

Is there a reasonable ratio of software to hardware?

In other words, are you getting economic use from some expensive machine?

Should you buy more software to use with it or would it be better to write off, sell or exchange some pieces of equipment no one wants to use?

Similarly if you are considering buying an expensive machine are you sure it will receive sufficient use to justify the outlay?

Can you afford enough compatible software to make it an economical investment?

Does a piece of equipment you are considering have a record of reliability? Ask advice from your local education authority, your teachers' centre or other schools. Do not take the manufacturer's word for it. The Council for Educational Technology will supply user specifications free and technical reports compiled by the Test Bureau (Training & Educational Systems Testing Bureau) are available from many LEAs.

Is the machine's necessary maintenance difficult or costly? Can it be operated only by someone with technical knowledge or is it really simple to use? Try it out on a few children and see how they manage. Ensure that anything bought for children's use is really suitable, eg, projectors with automatic focus.

Is the machine reasonably versatile? Beware of commercial samples of recording and visuals prepared for demonstration but which do not necessarily indicate how the machine will perform with other material. Try it out with home-made software where appropriate.

Will the machine work satisfactorily where you want to use it? Does it unnecessarily duplicate a resource already in the school?

Do you already have access (without too much time or travel) to a similar machine, eg can you easily use copiers or recorders in your local teachers' centre, or get work done for you quickly?

Buy the best microphone compatible with your recorders and the best quality tapes. Cassette tapes are made in different lengths: C60 (plays 60 minutes, 30 minutes each side) C90 (90 minutes, 45 minutes each side) and C120 (1 hour each side). If practical it is best to use a tape the same length as the item to be recorded. If several items are recorded on a large tape the wear caused by running the tape at high speed to reach the item needed (when it has been recorded after other items) is much heavier than the wear caused by actually playing the tape. This applies equally to video tape recording (VTR) and to video cassette recording (VCR).

Many local education authorities have quite precise rules for the purchase of hardware and make positive recommendations. Some issue a list of recommended hardware and will not authorize the purchase of anything else from local authority funds; in particular, no one should consider choosing their own microcomputer (even if they have the money) without reference to their LEA. The list is usually quite short and based in suitability and safety. Some authorities have a central store where recommended equipment is displayed and advice is available. Others issue schools with a standard 'package' of hardware considered adequate for the size of the school. This package does not always include duplicating or copying machines. Many authorities provide a good maintenance service and, generally speaking, the people best pleased with their maintenance service are those for whom the local education authority provides standard equipment recommendations or a package.

Maintenance and repair
A frequent cause of irritation and loss of faith in resource-based learning is the breakdown of some piece of equipment upon which a lesson is depending. This may 'only' mean a long wait until a spare bulb is found, but it may mean having to abandon the whole plan.

So it is important to have arrangements for immediate, urgent maintenance and repairs. Is there a stock of spare bulbs, etc, and does everyone know where it is?

The wise teacher checks the working of a piece of equipment beforehand!

Is there someone in the school who can diagnose faults and repair them? Most staffs include someone with the necessary expertise. One head referred to a teacher who had 'been on a course' and can

46

now 'mend some hardware and set it up'. Another spoke of using an 'overworked technician' and a third had an 'audio resource centre assistant' who could do some repairs. At any rate some 'pre-crisis' allocation of responsibility is required.

There are various regional arrangements for hardware repairs, some a good deal more reliable than others. Almost all schools have the chance of using some central repair service but many complained of the difficulty of making contact with the right person and also of long delays before items were returned.

Provided that there is no local rule against it, and so no problem involved in paying out school money, contact with a friendly electronics business is a good idea. Some schools are very happy with this local service and get quick attention. Perhaps some technically qualified parent would be glad to cooperate *provided it does not contravene your maintenance contract.*

Availability
Another cause of irritation over hardware is the question of availability. It really is essential to have a system for booking larger pieces of equipment. There is likely, for instance, to be only one movie projector in the school and so its use must be planned ahead. It is a good idea to have certain basic items of hardware in each classroom or teaching area. Provided of course such an arrangement is cost effective in terms of use, the equipment is carefully maintained and can be securely stored away outside school hours. If such items as tape recorders and playbacks, slide viewers and loop projectors are instantly available all day, only heavier, larger items will need to be booked ahead.

Someone must be in charge of the bookings and the system must be rigidly respected. For example, if TV sets are used as VDUs it is very important to keep careful records. Programmes are broadcast at specific times and it is no use Mr Y expecting to borrow the TV set to use as a VDU with a microcomputer when Miss X wants to record a nature programme. Purpose-built VDUs are rapidly becoming cheaper and cheaper to buy and a school aware of the potential of information technology will hopefully have acquired one for each microcomputer that it possesses. However, most primary schools are likely to have only one microcomputer and this must be monitored very rigidly. Many schools have an 'a-v book', kept in the staffroom, and teachers fill in for the appropriate day what they want and at what time. One school has a large washable board, like a kitchen memo board, hung at the storage point of each piece of equipment. Teachers write their requests on the board and the notes are erased once the occasion is past.

A monthly wall calendar is an invaluable aid to planning ahead.

First thing every morning it must be someone's duty to take what has been booked to where it is required for that day. This is done sometimes by ancillaries, but can be done by capable trained children. They should work in pairs to facilitate the handling of heavier equipment and should of course receive proper instruction in the elementary precautions of taking care of hardware — and themselves.

Transportation of large hardware, even on a trolley, can be a problem, especially in schools with staircases between classrooms. Television sets and microcomputers should be available to as many classes, groups of pupils and individuals as possible. A microcomputer, in particular, should be highly portable to enable teachers to take it home to practise on as they are unlikely to have time during school hours.

Some trusting schools have hardware freely displayed on large tables and anything not previously reserved can be taken and used. However, most people keep portable equipment locked in a cupboard or strong room, especially after school hours.

A list of hardware available for loan should be circulated among the staff and regularly brought up to date. Each piece of equipment should have a record card which describes it and gives its price and date of acquisition. This should indicate who has it on loan. On returning it the borrower should record any faults found.

The card will also be a record of repairs done, spares supplied, and can be withdrawn while an item is away for major repairs. This list will provide an added check on things away for a long period.

All this may seem excessive zeal to those with only a small stock of hardware, but the stock will grow. Also, it is always better to have detailed records of anything, whether it is a book or a complicated electronic device, which is going to be used by several people in several places.

Miscellaneous reminders
Loose electrical leads are required to connect hardware with the mains supply and the tidiest, easiest way to store these is hanging on a large hook on the wall. Different types of connections are needed to fit different types of hardware (and sometimes different types of plugs at the *other* end). By using a colour code, (paint or plastic label) for each type of connection the right lead can be distinguished at a glance. The same colour should appear at the connection end of the lead and at the insertion point in the item of equipment. For stereo equipment it is advisable to mark every right-hand channel connection (both on equipment and on leads) with some invariable identification code — (or left-hand, of course, but *not* both).

Small items (hand viewers, cameras, etc) can be locked away in filing cabinets, cupboards or deep drawers. Large equipment needs a special store room, or even a strong room specially reinforced. Break-ins are becoming more and more common, especially into single-storey schools and the thieves' target is usually electronic equipment. Painting the school's name on items is no deterrent and burglars show growing ingenuity in evading normal defence devices. So security is of paramount importance in hardware storage.

Only a few selected items of hardware can be recommended for use in the library/resource centre. These can be defined as those which cause the minimum of disturbance to other users.

ROPS-D

Audio listening stations with headphones distract no one else. Some listening stations can take 2 inputs, or all the children can listen to the same programme.

Slide viewing by individuals is as peaceful an occupation as reading, small group viewing is no more disturbing than small group teaching, or reading round a table. A work top about 2ft 6in wide, backed by a screen, or vertical panel, painted matt white, provides a convenient way for more than one child to look at the same material.

Using a microcomputer, for input or output, can be quite unobtrusive if done by a trained operator. However, untrained children should not be allowed to regard it as a toy and use it unattended.

An induction loop fitted in a classroom enables several children to listen on headphones, without disturbing others, and the absence of leads gives total freedom of movement. An induction loop could be fitted in the library/resource centre without inhibiting its use by other people. Headphones are popular with children, but such equipment must, of course, be fitted by a qualified electrician.

Activities (viewing or listening) which involve larger groups of children and totally disrupt the legitimate use of the library/ resource centre must not be tolerated. Proper provision of television aerial sockets and power points in teaching areas should obviate the need to use the library for either television or film viewing. Schools with video cassette recorders may use television more effectively by a wired distribution system to several classrooms.

Film viewing may need blackout so at least one classroom should have suitable curtains or blinds and be freed occasionally by timetabling to provide for large group viewing of films.

In some authorities we find the provision of a special carpeted room with good acoustics, adequate seating space, television aerial and power points. This room could be used for all group viewing and could double up as a recording studio or for drama rehearsals.

Both these solutions may sound too idealistic to a crowded school. But it must be emphasized that some arrangement must be devised to protect the library from domination by one group to the total exclusion of the rest of the school and the virtual closure of the library.

Storage of materials: some general suggestions
Many resources can be stored on open shelves, eg film loops, video cassettes and 8mm or 16mm film. But, although they can be stored like books, they cannot be browsed through in the same way and must be carefully labelled with title and subject content. This is especially true of video cassettes which often contain several programmes.

It is difficult to store resources securely without making access more difficult (keys have a malicious habit of disappearing) but it is necessary to keep some items locked away, especially if the school is used for other activities in the evenings.

Containers need to be easily used by young children who often find drawers difficult, and for whom many commercially produced storage units are too high. The top drawers of a four-drawer filing cabinet, for instance, are too high for the average primary child. There should never be any excuse for climbing on a shelf, or standing on a chair, to reach materials.

Furniture in constant use must be durable enough to stand up to continual battering without falling apart, but there is also something to be said for cheap convenient storage of a more ephemeral nature which can be replaced cheaply. Units made of polythene, or strong card, are commercially available and these are both portable and adaptable.

When choosing storage units, there are some safety rules to remember. Four-drawer metal cabinets will tip over if the top two drawers are opened together. They should therefore be bolted to the floor, as should free-standing shelves. Free-standing shelving is an open temptation to a small child to stand on a lower shelf to reach a higher one. Any plastic bags used as containers must have the corner cut off, so no very small objects can be kept in plastic bags. Some commercially produced furniture has sharp corners or may develop jagged edges as the result of rough handling.

Bearing all these points in mind, it is still worth looking widely around at all kinds of possible furniture (much of it not intended for libraries at all).

There are on the market nowadays some interesting room dividers with interchangeable drawers and shelves. In the home they divide trendy kitchen from elegant sitting room, but in a library they can be used to bring all kinds of media together, and placed in a central position will break up floor space without excluding light.

Two sided trolleys are mobile and can be used also as temporary room dividers. Conventional book trolleys have long been used to

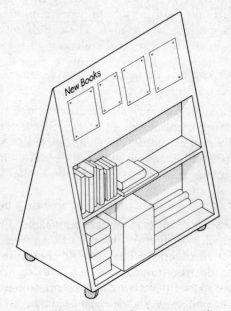

Figure 3. Trolley with shelves and display space

52

collect up books needed for a particular topic and move them from a central point to a classroom.

But there are now trolleys available with pinboard backing, with shelves and slopes and ledges, all ideal for moving multi-media collections or providing temporary displays.

There are several commercial storage units, designed to store every kind of audio-visual material together, including some print items. Flexiform supply a standard frame from which you can choose your own internal fittings. Terrapin Reska market audio-visual media storage furniture which comes in one or two cabinet units — these are as adaptable as Flexiform and cheaper. They can be wired to a 13-amp socket to provide a light for inspecting slides, etc. Don Gresswell too sell units for multi-media storage. These are only three examples in a growing market. You should be sure you cannot devise your own storage units before you decide to buy a commercially produced one. You will need to consider the cost in terms of what else the money could buy and also be sure you have space for something which may be as large as a wardrobe.

Much office furniture is perfectly adaptable to school use. Notably, of course, filing cabinets which are solid and lockable. The two-drawer type is better for primary schools than the four-drawer. Not only because the four-drawer can be a hazard, but also because two-drawer cabinets can be put under a working surface, or two together will provide a worktop, or a display surface, at a reasonable height for young children.

Card cabinets for 5in X 3in record cards can easily be adapted to store smaller items like cassettes and filmstrips. Sometimes school secretaries have these surplus to requirements owing to some change in record-keeping procedures. It is certainly worth asking!

There are various types of shelving you might consider, if your local authority gives you any choice. Balmforth, Terrapin Reska, Ladderax and Libraco can all be used either as free-standing units, or as wall shelving. All the modern shelving systems provide deeper shelving which will accommodate filing boxes and other storage units which will not fit on standard shelves.

There are numerous sizes and varieties of what are generally called 'tidy boxes'. Some are standard issue for infant schools from the authority's central store, others are specially made. Some are small enough to take slides, others large enough for multi-media topic loans, but all are strongly made with lids. Shirt boxes are perfectly adequate substitutes for tidy boxes, but they are not quite so strong. They are however usually free, provided some obliging suppliers can be found. The snag is that neither shirt boxes nor tidy boxes will fit neatly on to standard shelves.

Boxes which originally contained carbon paper or typing paper are a handy size and can be used in numberless ways. It is worth considering domestic containers and shop fittings in the context of multi-media storage. The average supermarket can be a source of ideas and the various ways of storing wallpaper could be adapted to chart and picture storage. Dubonnet is sold from deep cartons with detachable cardboard divisions. These are rubbish to the wine merchants, but could be ideal for small maps, charts and pictures!

Plastic lunch boxes are convenient containers for kits: they will take a cassette or filmstrip and notes. The boxes pile neatly on top of each other on a normal library shelf.

Cornflake packets are as ubiquitous as shirt boxes and a great deal more adaptable. They fit neatly onto library shelves and can be cut up three ways to serve different purposes:

A. Provides two containers for small items or reel tapes with notes. There is room on the front edge for Dewey numbers and list of contents.

B. Makes a standard shaped pamphlet box. This is not quite so strong as commercially produced pamphlet boxes but pasting brown paper on the outside makes it stronger. Thick wallpaper will also add strength and make the boxes more attractive for classroom use.

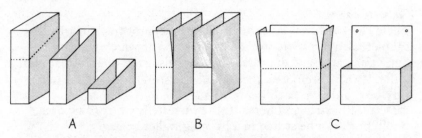

Figure 4. Cornflake packets cut in three different ways to make storage boxes

C. Can be pinned on to a shelf thus providing a hanging container for workcards or small items.

To attach labels to drawers and other containers, use double-sided adhesive tape. It adheres very strongly. Transparent melamine tape (also called non-shrink tape) is better than Scotch tape or Sellotape for covering numbers on books or containers (or indeed for small repairs), it does not go gummy and yellow.

All attempts at multi-media storage have to decide on some degree of separation of media. Shelving items together, on a subject basis, has been tried but in many ways this is not practical. So the next section will discuss storage based on the physical characteristics of media. It is by no means a comprehensive, definitive list of suggestions; many other ideas will be found in schools around the United Kingdom.

What follows are some suggestions of ways media and objects can be stored and some comments which may give you ideas of your own. Domestic containers in particular can be adapted for many more uses.

Storage of materials: medium by medium

Tapes – reel
These will go neatly into open-fronted pamphlet boxes with their notes tucked in beside them.

55

Cassette tapes

These can be stored individually in plastic inset trays in a Bisley cabinet, also in plastic storage trays, some of which will fit in 5in X 3in catalogue drawers. There are also free-standing carousel units. If there are notes, they should be stored with the cassette: a tidy box will take both items, or a common combination — cassette, filmstrip and notes. If the cassette is a recording of a book, both can be stored in a hanging wallet or bag.

Records

These are fragile and it is advisable to keep them away from the work areas, and use them as master copies for cassette recordings. However, it must not be forgotten that records can only be legally copied if your local education authority has taken out a licence for the purpose under the copyright provision. (See *Copyright*, CET Information Sheet 6, 1985, *Copyright and Education*, CET Working Paper 8, 1974, and *Copyright Clearance*, CET Guidelines 2, 1981.) If you want to encourage browsing, put the sleeves in a Librex browser box, or a Kinderbox (which is meant for picture books). Records on shelves need to be firmly supported with dividers. 'Racking units' from an office supplier interlock firmly and are very suitable.

Compact discs

These are smaller and tougher than records and are only damaged by greasy hands or dirt. They come in liners inside a rigid container and should be stored within this, in a suitable box. The sleeves can be used for browsing if they are put inside a PVC cover to preserve them.

Floppy discs

Microcomputer floppy discs need more care as careless handling can ruin them. They should be kept, clearly labelled, in purpose-designed envelopes and in a lockable storage case. Like video cassettes, they must be stored away from magnets, large motors, cathode ray tubes, direct sunlight, radiators and heating or cooling ducts. Never write on the label with a ball-point pen (this will damage the playing surface), only lightly with a felt tip. Never, never touch the exposed recording surface and always put a disc back into its envelope as soon as you remove it from the disc drive. Each piece of information occupies such a tiny spot that small scratches, dust or tobacco ash can make the information unusable. More detailed and technical advice will be supplied with the disc by the manufacturer. Study this carefully.

Slides/transparencies
These are very often stored in sets in packs with the teacher's notes in a pocket or at the back. Viewpacks, for example, are made of transparent polythene and consist of several small pockets attached to one side of a sheet, with a larger pocket for notes at the back. These packs fit into any ordinary filing cabinet and literally hundreds can be suspended in each drawer.

To examine slides, the whole pack can be held up to the light, or laid on a light box. Each slide should be numbered and linked by some code to the set, so checking for missing slides and replacing slides in the right pack should be easy. Plastic view packs can also be hung in the library from rods or spurshelving bars. This certainly makes for easy browsing, but does expose the slides to meddling fingers. Ricket book wallets are probably better than Viewpacks for sets of slides that are going to be loaned. Each wallet can contain a set of slides and notes and several will go neatly into a pamphlet box. Individual slides, which must of course be numbered and indexed, can be stored in film slide trays on a shelf or in a shallow drawer. Plastic slide cases, locked by a slide-to plastic labelled carrier, will stand on a shelf like a thin book. Boots' slide boxes will stack together and make a unit of several plastic drawers.

If compatible with the school's needs, slides can of course be kept in loading magazines in sets and sequences ready for projection.

Filmstrips and film loops
There is some conflict here between the usage pupils prefer and the convenience of adults. Some teachers find filmstrips tiresome and prefer to convert them to slides retaining only stories in filmstrip format. Slides can be selected from a sequence to suit a particular lesson and there are other advantages plain to adults.

But children like filmstrips and learn easily from film loops, if they are allowed to repeat them until they really understand what is being demonstrated.

Filmstrips labelled with a Dewey number should not be stored in Dewey order as this means adjusting drawer space every time a new one is added. It is better to add a running number to the Dewey number, thus the latest addition is added to the end of a sequence. The catalogue card will show media code, Dewey number and a running number, eg FS/598/194.

Filmstrips, in their containers, can be stored in Bisley units, in any small drawers fitted with lift-out dividers or in filmstrip trays on a shelf.

Overhead projector transparencies
These can be stored one behind the other in a filing cabinet, provided they are mounted in individual cardboard frames. Francis Gregory's 'Transaid' yellow mounts are thicker and more rigid than 3M mounts. But 3M mounts will fit into a standard-size filing cabinet; the others are larger and need Jumbo-size cabinets to accommodate them. A linked series can be titled and numbered together. Teaching notes can be either on the borders or on a sheet interleaved between transparencies.

Many audio-visual media storage units have suspended filing suitable for overhead projector transparencies and there are also albums for storing unmounted transparencies.

Of course, mounted overhead projector transparencies can perfectly well be stored in cardboard cartons and before buying expensive equipment for storage it is worth considering the transparencies' intrinsic value. Some will be too personal to be of general use. Only add those of good quality to the permanent library stock. Most commercially produced overhead projector transparencies are of good quality and will have been chosen for an educational programme.

Learning packs
These are now available, each containing teachers' notes, micro-

computer disc and audio cassette. The containers, a convenient size to go on shelves, must be clearly labelled and shelved in a meaningful order compatible with subject indexing. Care must be taken not to keep such packs near to heat or magnetic fields which can damage the microcomputer disc.

Work packs
These, for science experiments, etc, should be kept in plastic bags, either hung in a drawer or inside another container. The contents must be clearly listed and checked each time the pack is returned.

Kits
Small kits (eg, cassette, filmstrip and notes, or any combination of small items) will go nicely into stacking plastic lunch boxes. Topic loans need larger boxes. Cadging from shops or from parents may produce enough boxes, but they will be of various shapes and sizes. Large tidy boxes are probably stronger and better. It is possible to have large, deep topic boxes made to order, at a price.

Mobile tray units are also useful for storing all kinds of small software items and they fit easily under tables or benches. Individual trays can be taken out and used as containers for specially requested multi-media collections.

Charts
Large charts, maps and pictures are very difficult to store, especially if space is limited. Some way has to be found of making them accessible, visible and protected from damage. There are some ingenious manufactured storage units available, but none are cheap and some are quite prohibitively expensive.

For this section, large charts may be defined as printed sheets measuring about 27in × 40in (698mm × 1016mm). Anything smaller will be dealt with in the paragraph headed 'Pictures'.

Possible methods of storing the large sheets are by hanging, rolling, folding, or lying flat in map chests. Undoubtedly the best way is by individual suspension which allows for browsing and ensures that the chart does not get creased by handling, provided it is laminated. To laminate charts you can cover them yourself with Takibak, Vistafoil or similar transparent covering. The edges need to be bound by using an edge binder which secures overlapping tape round the chart. All charts, however stored, should have a hole punched at each corner to prevent the indiscriminate use of drawing pins. These holes can be reinforced with adhesive rings, as are used for pages in a ring binder. Stronger still are the metal reinforced holes made with 'Eyelet pliers' which can be bought at the sewing counters of most large shops.

Junior Books supply charts and large pictures already encased in a fitted envelope of transparent plastic and with reinforced holes. The cost is of course more than buying the chart direct, but should be weighed against the time and labour involved in doing the job yourself.

Hanging: commercial racks and rails often hang the charts too high for young children and nearly all, although good for browsing, making extracting a single chart difficult. For instance, Normidaire has metal holders of varying length and between 10 and 40 items can be suspended from each holder, depending on thickness. Browsing is easy, but the whole contraption needs space, preferably in a corner, and extracting charts is for adults only. The danger is that ten or eleven charts can fall out when only one is required. Units in the Elite range are very satisfactory, but costly.

There are two ingenious ways of utilizing items which may already be in the school and using them for chart storage. Metal rods can be run into the mesh of two wire mesh screens. First thread bulldog clips on to the rods, place the screens near enough to each other for the rods to be secure. The number of rods depends on how many charts you have; each chart is clipped and hung, browsing is easy, so is the removal of individual charts, but the arrangement takes up a great deal of space, and, for young children who might play around the area, is probably not stable enough.

Mobile cloakrooms will adapt for chart storage and they are on castors, so can be moved around at will. Wires are fixed across the frame (which is designed to take coat hangers) and charts are hung on bulldog clips, previously threaded on the wires.

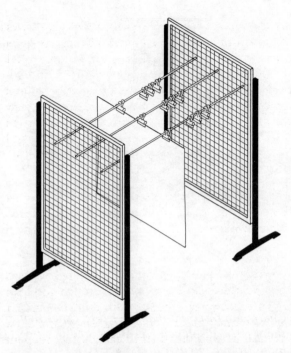

Figure 5. Chart hung by bulldog clips from rods extended between two wire mesh screens

Handy Angles or Dexion can be combined with hardboard, angle strips at each end provide a ledge on which to rest suspension rods. Similarly, a metal framework will provide support for bamboo canes, such as gardeners use, which are cheaper than metal rods. Fine plastic sheeting can be bought in long tubes (like an endless, bottomless plastic bag) and a suitable length stapled to the top of each chart. The cane is slipped through the chart which then hangs down inside the metal frame. Each chart is numbered or classified and can be arranged in any order compatible with the retrieval system. It is a simple matter to lift cane and chart out of the frame. When a chart is borrowed, the cane is left on the frame and the chart rehung when it is returned.

Another way of hanging charts does away with using drawing pins at all. They are mounted on sugar paper, with a few inches of

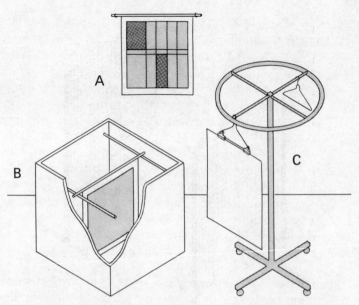

Figure 6. *Charts mounted on paper fixed to canes that enable them to be displayed (A) and stored in a box (B). Charts hung from a circular dress rack (C).*

paper spare at the top of the chart. The paper is folded over a rod and secured at the back of the chart with sellotape. The rod protrudes a few inches each side of the chart (see A). When not in use, the charts are hung on the rods inside a chest, each end of the rod resting on an angle bracket fitted inside the chest (see B). Each class-room has two hooks on a wall, spaced to take the ends of the rods so that the chart is hung on the classroom wall.

Circular dress racks take up very little space and charts can be hung from the radial rods by using loops of string and bulldog clips. But the charts have to be folded at least once or they will be too wide. This system is applicable only to the largest charts. Others are probably better rolled.

It is possible to take the doors off a wardrobe, fit the rods inside, hang wire coathangers on the rods and clip charts on to these with clothes pegs.

Hanging or rolling charts are both more satisfactory than trying to store them flat. Architects' plan chests, which open from the front, include the advantages of hanging, but the charts have to be taken out to be examined. The chests are expensive and only a few schools use them, though they are common enough in teachers' centres. In some, charts are secured on rods; in others, the charts are filed between corrugated dividers which prevent them slipping down.

One authority has created a chart trolley made from a tubular frame with laminated chipboard sides, forming a kind of trough with sides and no ends. The trolley runs on castors and is low enough for small children to use. The charts are mounted on strawboard and kept in large polythene bags. When placed in the unit they can be turned over like the pages of a book.

Charts can be folded to a manageable size and kept in drawers or containers, but the longer they remain folded, the less easy they are to display, because they refuse to hang flat without extra

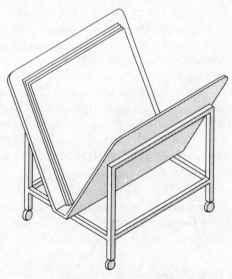

Figure 7. Chart trolley

pinning. Charts can also be stored flat in map chests but, even if the front of the drawers are hinged, retrieval of the charts is difficult and it is hard not to damage them. If the drawers are not hinged at the front this method can only be condemned as unworkable! It takes two people to extract a chart, since at least four hands are needed to lift up the pile and pull it out.

Rolling: charts rolled up and secured with rubber bands can be kept in umbrella stands, deep cartons or even garden incinerators. Wallpaper shops display rolls of paper in deep wire baskets. The Dewey number or other coding can be written on the back of the chart. Any box 24in (610mm) high will take eight rolled charts and the box can be covered with Fablon, or something similar. If there are several charts referring to related subjects (eg animals and birds) this can be indicated on the box. Such a box could be put at the end of the bookcase containing related books.

Rolled charts can also be kept in cardboard tubes. Alternatively, it is possible to buy transparent plastic tubes which have white cardboard caps at each end on which numbers can be written. If the charts are rolled with the picture on the outside, it is possible to have a glimpse of the material without taking the chart out of the tube. This method is especially useful for charts which are often lent, as they can be carried to classrooms still in their tubes. Triangular-shaped tubes are also available. Charts are easily taken out of these and this shape means that many charts can be stored horizontally on a deep shelf, or in a cupboard. Tubes are better stored upright to prevent them rolling about. However rolled charts are stored, it is essential to be able to handle them freely and have space to make additions without the need to reorganize the whole collection.

One disadvantage of storing charts by rolling them is that they refuse to unroll and threaten to engulf a small child. The struggle to flatten them can easily result in damage to chart — or child!

'Paper Pots' are tubs on castors which are designed to store sugar paper in a circular arrangement. The inside of the pot is filled with

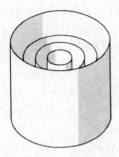

Figure 8. A 'Paper Pot'

concentric dividers and individual pieces of paper are easily
extracted by children. The device is large and the paper comes out
hardly folded at all so it is used for chart storage in some schools.
It is bulky and takes only a limited number of charts, being really
designed for sheets of paper.

If your method of storing charts is one that makes retrieval very
difficult, and you are not able to change it, it is worth having
small, manageable reproductions of the charts for people to
browse through and make their choice. Someone clever with a
camera can take photographs of the charts and produce:

(a) coloured slides: these have the advantage of indicating the use
of colour in the poster
(b) photographs which can be kept in a ring binder on the library
shelves. A good black-and-white photograph measuring 20cm X
30cm is large enough to read the print on most posters.

Obviously, whichever method is chosen, the charts and the reproductions must be clearly linked by numbering or some other code.

Pictures and small charts
These can be rolled and stored in containers with dividers (like the
Dubonnet box described) or they can be hung by pegging them
with clothes pegs to wires across a large box.

Smaller pictures can be stored in filing cabinets, either mounted on cardboard and arranged by subject heading (or Dewey numbers) or put in manila files arranged in the same way. It is only worth mounting pictures you really want to keep. Others should be cut out, put in manila files, and given away for illustrations for topics. This is a useful end for pictures from discarded books. Some schools make very large folders and fill them with all kinds of pictures, maps and small charts, keeping the folders in a store cupboard.

Most audio-visual aids storage units have suspended filing which can be used for pictures, pamphlets, etc. Postcards are often of increasing historical interest. They can be kept in slide wallets or in plastic single wallets. It is probably best not to involve them with other pictorial material. They have a social significance of their own.

Print materials
Jackdaws will file in order in a filing cabinet, the alternatives being cardboard cartons, or heaps on the shelves. So if you make your own Jackdaw-like collections of print materials, keep the container small enough to file conveniently. Newspaper cuttings and single sheets are best kept in flat boxes unless they are worth mounting and filing for long-term use. Pamphlets, etc, can go in lateral hanging files such as Railex or fittings inside a multi-media storage unit, etc. Triumph design holds lateral files and closes up

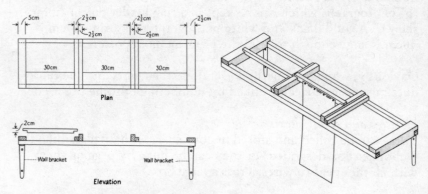

Figure 9. A method of storing stencils

with a folding blind that pulls down over all. Stencils must be hung carefully as it is easy to distort the holes in the top so that the stencil slips when put into the duplicator. One school has devised its own effective way of storing stencils. (See Figure 9.)

Lawco make a portable stencil cabinet and so do Roneo. Both are cheap and efficient.

Models, specimens and realia
Mobile tray units are useful for storing smaller items. Collections of small, disparate objects can go in open-fronted pamphlet boxes. Shells and pebbles (or other not very fragile objects) can be hung in plastic bags on rods in a filing cabinet.

Video tapes and video cassettes
These stand easily on ordinary library shelves, but must be stored well away from heat or any magnetic field. Their contents should be clearly listed on the outside of the container, because it is hardly worth including them in the library catalogue, as they will so often be erased and used again.

Methods of identification

Subject coding

Items in a library resource centre are containers of facts. The surest way of losing anything is to put it back in the wrong place, so in dealing with hundreds of items we have to decide on a code not only to help us find things but also to be sure we put them back in the right place. In this context the binding of a book is as much a container as the box for slides, the wallet for postcards or the tube for a chart.

Ordinary things can be arranged by their physical characteristics but it is the contents of a book or cassette that matter. Some physical separation may be forced upon us for practical reasons. Because of their varying sizes and shapes it is not ideal to shelve all media relating to one subject in the same place. Even the organizers of collections used by responsible adults have trouble with this procedure. One famous teachers' centre works with multi-media shelving and up to a point it helps, but the overall effect is untidy and sometimes startling. As when one is confronted by the cold hard stare of a stuffed owl in the section classified 598.2 (birds). One very large exhibition stock of audio-visual materials, used only by teachers and other interested adults is by considered choice arranged by physical form of media (centrally catalogued) even though there are no books to complicate matters.

Although some physical separations of media are forced upon the organizers of school library/resource centres we must not lose sight of the subject approach. Obviously some people will prefer using one kind of media rather than another, that is understandable. But it has to be said that although the basis of a library/resource centre must be an organized collection of books, properly classified, there are teachers who still need convincing that information retrieval can be done from all media using the same techniques.

Experience has proved that the most effective way of arranging books is to divide them into story books and information books. Story books are most often arranged on the shelves in alphabetical order of author's surnames, but there are other ways of encouraging and helping children to find suitable stories and these will be discussed later. Information books should be arranged in broad subject groupings with some form of code on the spine of the book so that it can be quickly found and replaced correctly.

There is a strong case for using the same code for audio-visual material.

Children can appreciate a logical arrangement of books from an early age. Obviously at the nursery age attractive display is paramount, but even then picture books by the same artists can be grouped together. At the infant stage attractive displays are still important but we can begin to group information books together according to their subject content. This can be done very simply by colour coding so that for instance all the books on trees have green labels on their spines and all the books on cars have yellow ones. The children can be encouraged to return books to the right place and will quickly learn the colour used for subjects they are interested in. This applies to software too of course.

You are strongly advised to base your subject groupings on the foundation of the Dewey Decimal Classification. This has proved its worth over many years and is used in all British public libraries so a child needs to become familiar with the basic principles as soon as possible.

Many people find the whole structure of the Dewey Decimal Classification daunting and confusing. Others find it much too rigid. But it has survived and proved its worth for a very long time, and is adaptable. Using numbers for identification,

70

knowledge is divided into ten main classes which are in turn sub-divided to accommodate specific subjects. There is no need to use more than three digits even in junior libraries. The main grouping is logical and your choice should follow the same pattern.

When it comes to classifying junior books or other materials it is perfectly reasonable to adapt Dewey, provided the relationships implied in the tables are clearly understood. For instance, there is a section 'Biography', number 920: for children biographies are probably better with the subject associated with the person concerned than in some subdivision of 920, eg, Pasteur with medicine, Stephenson with railways or Brunel with bridges. There are two possible places for books about trains; one is the transport section (385) and one is the engineering section (625). A decision must be made about which number to use and all the relevant items given the same number. This will be indicated on the subject index. Dewey also makes a distinction between the history and the geography of a country. It makes more sense to put all children's books about a country at the history number since most of them will deal with a country's past in the context of its present — the numbers will be simpler and shorter too because of the way the section is subdivided.

Such adaptations work well, provided they are consistently adhered to. What will not work is mangling Dewey: taking blocks of numbers out and reworking them to your own design. The whole structure is too logical for that.

For many years, the School Library Association's *Introduction to Dewey Decimal Classification* has guided teachers and librarians in making these decisions. Revised in 1977 and again in 1985, this publication is an essential tool for anyone intending to classify resources in a logical and professionally acceptable way.

Home-made classification schemes will not work either. Someone with a small collection may cheerfully start by devising their own scheme, based, for instance on letters of the alphabet. Such a scheme may work for a while but more than one experience has proved the inherent disaster in such ventures, especially as the library grows larger. Besides, standardization with the local library, indeed with the entire network of national libraries, has advantages too numerous to list.

The person colour coding books for infants needs to have access to a simplified version of the Dewey classification as there has to be a clear, consistent progression, from colours-only for infants to colour-plus-numbers for juniors. Juniors accustomed to this labelling can easily make the transition to Dewey numbers only, which is what they will find in their secondary school and public library. To give an example: a book on money simple enough for a six-year-old will have a coloured label only. A book on money for juniors will have the same coloured label plus the number 330, which is the Dewey number for money. The stock in the junior school will be larger and the children's demands more specific so more detailed subject grouping is required.

Colour coding is a valuable aid not only for children. The library in one of our newer universities uses colour coding to indicate subject areas. There are five floors in the library and each is characterized by a different colour scheme. Floor coverings, curtains and woodwork are all painted to match. In the entrance hall is the key.

1st floor	Reception and reference	White
2nd floor	Science	Yellow
3rd floor	Sociology	Red
4th floor	History, geography, philosophy	Blue
5th floor	Literature, language, arts	Green

The student glides up in an open-fronted lift and knows exactly where to step off. Our infant, nurtured on colour coding, is going to feel quite at home in this library.

But to return to the infant library where the books are similarly coded and arranged in broad subject divisions...

Too few colours mean very broad divisions and will lead to a child having to hunt through what may seem to him to be a miscellaneous collection of books unrelated to what he wants.

The following example used in an infant school employs only 5 colours.

Bible stories	White
Transport	Yellow
Science	Green
Poetry and dictionaries	Red
Countries and people	Blue

Such a scheme has serious omissions and would need a detailed, carefully devised subject index to make it work. Subject indexes are described later. The whole concept of so few colours may have been intended to simplify the arrangement of materials but it really defeats its own ends. The subject divisions are at one and the same time too wide and too narrow. To devote a whole section to Bible stories and only one to science is not a balanced approach. Surely, even for a young child, natural science must be separated from applied science. In another school someone has devised a scheme with 7 divisions, but similar criticisms can be made of that.

Many varied colour codes have been devised but most schemes, dividing subject content into arbitrary groups, share serious disadvantages. We cannot expect a perfect match with Dewey but a colour code should be based on the framework of the Dewey scheme. This ensures the progress in understanding that has already been described.

The table on the following page suggests a system which links colour coding to the Dewey Classification. The groupings are approximately those in the classification schedule and even at the first steps the child will have some idea of where to begin looking. It has been used successfully in several London primary schools and can be recommended. It can be applied to all media, it is not intended only for books. It is a subject approach which cuts across the media barrier and however your materials are separated by physical characteristics you should be able to apply this simple system.

Do not take the choice of colours as obligatory. If you already

ADULT TERMS	CHILDREN'S TERMS	COLOUR	DEWEY NUMBER
Reference Books	Encyclopædias Finding out	White	000
Religion	Bible stories Gods of other lands	Pink	220 290
Services Communications	People who help us Jobs Cars, ships, trains Aircraft	Yellow	360 380
Language	ABC Words Dictionaries	White	420
Natural science	Our world Numbers Plants Animals	Green Black Green Green	500 510 580 590
Applied science	Machines Building	Purple	620 690
Arts Sports	Handicraft Music Sports	Pale blue	740 780 790
Literature	Nursery rhymes Poetry Plays	Orange	 821 822
Geography	People in other countries	Brown	910 Exploration 912 Maps 940-99
History	People before us	Red	920-930

A table to show the link between simple colour coding and the Dewey Decimal Classification use a colour code, and are happy with it, do not change. The juxtaposition of colours is important and the last three colours on this list, which will of course be in blocks next to one another, are really too alike. Some pinks and oranges are not easily distinguished. Also red can fade to pink and the books be returned to the wrong place. In addition we are told that one in eight male human beings is colour blind. So this coupled with fading labels on the sunny side of the library can certainly cause problems.

A worse situation is created if there is no collaboration concerning the choice of colours for subject content in linked infant and junior schools. Of course not all junior schools use colours so the transition for the child may be from broad subject groups, colour coded, to more detailed subject groupings with numbers. The colour coding in his infant school has accustomed him to subject groups, so he should not find this too difficult. However, if the junior school uses colour coding plus Dewey numbers as many do, it is very confusing to look for white labels, expecting to find encyclopædias and instead find Bible stories. It cannot be urged too strongly that infant and junior head teachers should consult one another on the choice of colours for subject classification.

Before dealing with the indexing of materials to find individual items perhaps it is as well to touch on practical matters. Coloured plastic labels can be bought in packets from most large stationers, or you can buy coloured sticky paper and cut it up into small strips. If you buy these locally there is always the risk that your supplier will run out of stock of the colours you have chosen. Always buy labels or paper (and other stationery) from your local education authority regional supplier.

When it comes to adding numbers to coloured labels in the junior school Dymo marking is far and away the best method. The coloured tapes can be embossed with clear numbers. Writing on coloured labels is not very successful as a rule and two labels, one coloured and one numbered look messy. White, the best colour to write on, has probably been used in the subject coding so another neutral colour needs to be used.

Dymo labels do not fade as fast as paper ones, are slightly harder to pick off books and containers and can be used as shelf labels also. But they are not so flexible as labels on spines that have to bend, eg, paperbacks.

If the categories you have chosen become too broad, because your stock is becoming too large, you can of course subdivide by using a second colour. For instance the natural science section may quickly get too unwieldy even in an infant library. By adding another colour to the basic green you can separate books on animals from those on trees. But there are dangers in introducing too many colours. It is preferable to add the simplest Dewey number and so introduce quite young children to the idea of a number code. The purpose and logic of these numbers will be easily understood by a motivated child. Three possible examples are 520 for books on astronomy, 580 for books on plants and 590 for books on animals. The child will find what he wants very quickly and be a valuable step nearer understanding library organization.

Colour coding as a location guide — to tell the inquirer where the object he wants can be found — is of course closely involved with subject coding. Especially for books, as all your books on natural science, for instance, will have green labels and will be shelved together. Look for the green labels and you will find your nature study tapes and slides.

An open-plan school can have subject areas where you will find a multi-media collection, all colour coded alike. This system makes returning books and everything else to their home base a simple matter. It also means that, even if media are separated, the youngest child (who will certainly know whether he wants to look or listen!) can go to the place where the appropriate software is stored and choose an item marked with the right colour.

One school has developed this system so that it is perfectly relevant to all ages and abilities. Not only are the items of software coded with Dymo tape embossed with a Dewey number but the storage areas are also coloured. Pigeonholes or shelves are lined with paper of the appropriate colour. So there is really no excuse for anything to stray.

One open-plan school has discarded written records, except for stock taking, and relies on colour for subject grouping and information retrieval. Materials are grouped in five subject areas, not based on Dewey but quite logical. For instance one corner is called 'Living things' and has a large yellow card on the wall. There are also pictures of animals, birds and plants. The colour yellow is marked on everything in the resource collection that relates to living things. Much audio-visual material is not actually exhibited but is easily found in cupboards, being clearly marked yellow.

The card on the wall lists seven subdivisions of the 'Living things' section:
1   Animals
2   Birds
3   Reptiles and amphibians
4   Insects and spiders
5   Plants
6   Life in water
7   General books

The books are arranged in these groups and everything is easily seen or freely available. The children are free to wander round the school and find what they need. This really is reducing the organizing of resources to its simplest level. But such a system would be quite unworkable in a conventional school with separate class-rooms. It could of course be adapted, where applicable, in a version related to Dewey such as the colour code already suggested.

Subject index
An alphabetical subject index is the key to any arrangements of material, whether based on colour or number. A subject index is not a catalogue, it is a guide to inquirers telling them where to look for materials on a particular subject. If all materials are uniformly coded the inquirer knows that he looks for the code number (or colour) on book, cassette or whatever. A catalogue is a list of individual items, a catalogue tells the inquirer whether a

particular item is in the library, and where to find it. The subject index is also the key to the classified catalogue since an inquirer, once knowing the number of his subject, can either look and see what items are available or look in the classified/subject catalogue and find what items are in stock (even if they are out on loan).

If you wish you can indicate in the subject index whether the subject is covered by more than one medium. You need to devise a code that will not be confused with the subject code. Some forms of subject index are more suitable for this than others. On the whole it is best to keep the subject index as simple as possible, but you may want to encourage the multi-media approach in this way.

The relevance of the subject index is easily understood and can be used by children as soon as they can read at all. Pupils should be encouraged to suggest additional headings, or point out omissions. How one group of children helped to make their own subject index is described in the section on child helpers.

The simplest kind of subject index is a visible index on the wall of the resources centre. For infants this will be large cards with one simple word printed on them followed by the colour code. Juniors will need the Dewey number as well so their cards will look like this.

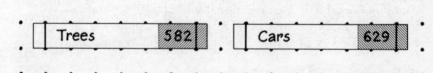

Figure 10. Colour-coded subject index cards with Dewey numbers

These cards must be cut out of strong cardboard which should be covered with transparent foil. The printing must be large enough to be read from several feet away, and by small children well below the level of the wall index, which is best fixed above the shelving. The cards must be arranged in alphabetical order

78

and should be secured in a way that makes additions and subtractions easy. Any kind of wall list, however large and beautiful the printing, is not suitable for a subject index. Cards can be moved, a list needs deletions, and insertions written in. Flexibility is achieved by either pinning the cards to a pinboard, or by threading elastic thread through the holes in pegboard and slotting cards into the loops.

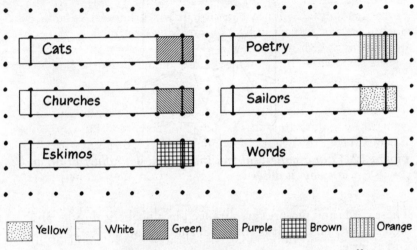

Figure 11. Colour-coded subject index cards on wall

There should not be too many cards, a few basic topics are enough for infants, and of course the terminology must be simple and appropriate to the age of the children: 'cars' not 'automobile engineering', 'police', 'firemen' or 'postmen', not 'public services'. Even for juniors too many cards are confusing, especially if they are arranged too closely together.

The cards should be arranged with clear divisions, or a large capital letter, between each letter group. This way the subject index is also serving the useful purpose of teaching the principles of alphabetical order, something which does not seem to be taught any more and which still defeats many adults.

A very attractive visible subject index can be made on pinboard fixed to the wall above the book stacks. Subjects like cars, police, weather are clearly printed on card: beside each card is a picture and next to that the Dewey number and colour code.

Figure 12. Colour-coded subject index card with illustration and Dewey number

These cards and pictures are arranged in alphabetical order and well spaced. The result is colourful and appropriate to all ages and abilities.

The pocket chart used with 'Breakthrough' reading scheme can also be used as a visible subject index: it will be infinitely flexible, and cards can be changed frequently and easily.

Stripdex can be used as yet another visible subject index. Its use, and how to make duplicate copies, are described in the section on organizing dispersed resources.

A subject index for the use of the coordinator can be made on 5in × 3in cards. This is added to by degrees, as new items are classified, and ensures consistency of classifying. There is no need to agonize more than once on what number to give a book on windmills, or hovercraft, or water pollution! You make a decision, record it and the next time there is no problem. Unless you are absolutely sure of a number it is always wise to consult your own subject index as well as the Dewey index. It is better to be consistent than to be a perfect classifier! The main thing is to keep related items together and to list them so that they can be found.

If you feel you would like to make a subject index on cards for everyone's use it will of course be a much more ambitious undertaking. If it is intended for general use it must cover all subject areas, not just the problem ones. It is however a very useful tool and provides an opportunity for teaching children how to use card indexes. But be very careful who you allow to use this index. Pupils need some instruction and boys especially have a genius for wrecking a carefully sorted card index in three destructive minutes! Most children enjoy using a card index but it can only be used by one at a time, or one per drawer, and it is essential to have a visible index too.

Colour coding as a physical form designator

The purpose of this use of colour is to indicate what media are available and link them to each subject or topic. This labelling of like media must not be confused with subject coding. Subject indications are also needed if the material is to be of any use. A collection of filmstrips, with a coloured label on each container, the same colour on the drawer or box and the whole labelled 'filmstrips', is quite useless. The individual items must also be subject coded. So there is a clear choice involved in the use of colour. Either you use colour to designate subjects, or to separate media: you cannot do both.

For media designation multi-media packs need more than one coloured label. A multi-media pack on birds could contain notes, slides and a cassette. So it is quite reasonable to put on the container 598 (the Dewey number for birds) plus the colours for cassettes and slides respectively. The problem now is where to shelve it!

Coding of media in the stock records can be done simply by filing all the index cards in subject order and then adding some codes on the card to indicate that the item is not a book. For

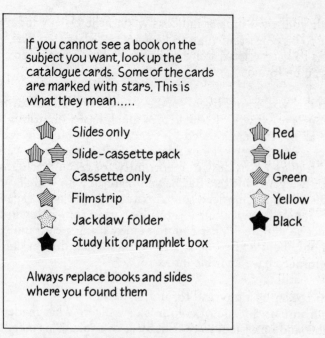

Figure 13. Key to media colour coding

young children brightly coloured stars or dots are attractive and easily understood.

A card displayed in one school explains this procedure very clearly. The colours are indicated by bright star-shaped labels, the card is an attractive greeny-grey and the whole written in beautiful script.

The scheme illustrated is very simple, the categories are very broad and there is no way of easily expanding the code to include newly acquired media such as computer software. However, computer software is very vulnerable and best kept away from untrained hands (see page 56).

It is useful to differentiate in stock records between materials which need a machine to exploit them, and books and other print material. Printed material will be listed on white cards and software on orange cards, or whatever. Some media code to indicate the type of software needs to be added. The inquirer is instantly alerted to the fact that what he wants demands a piece of equipment before he can use it. But this is probably only marginally more efficient than having everything recorded on cards of the same colour. To encourage the subject approach the coloured cards should be integrated into the same sequence as the cards for books.

A more complex development of the idea is to divide your media into groups and allocate a different coloured card for each group. It is best not to use too many colours — broad divisions are best.

Here are some suggestions:

Print form
Visual — still
Visual — moving
Audio
Three-dimensional — multi-media

Individual records of individual items, whether on coloured cards or coded in some other ways, can of course be filed separately by medium. Some teachers who have a real preference for one medium prefer this way of filing. But this cuts across the subject approach and may lead to a narrow approach to the material available on a topic.

Another code, also using only four colours, divides media up differently:

Printed material   — Black
Picture and slides — Red
Filmstrips   — Blue
Tapes   — Green

The colours are painted or labelled on the items and coloured stickers are on the record cards.

One way of applying and explaining such colour divisions is to have lists on coloured paper hung on the wall. For instance a large sheet of blue paper lists the subjects about which filmstrips are available. This is a very simple routine for information retrieval but has the disadvantage — inflexibility — of any written list. Alterations will soon make it look untidy.

Where different coloured cards are used in the card catalogue to indicate different media it is a good idea to stick specimens of the actual cards used on to a board hung over the card catalogue.

In one school blocks of numbers are allocated to different media as part of the information retrieval system. So the board over the catalogue has the relevant numbers opposite the coloured cards. The numbers are omitted here, but this is no reflection on the system which is completely efficient.

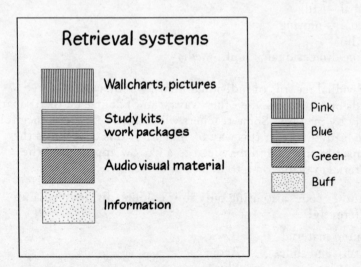

Figure 14. Board with cards as key to media colour coding, with space for numbers

Colour coding to indicate media can also be used with a *subject* index on a strip index panel. Strips can be of a uniform colour, with coloured spots added to indicate what media are available for the subject listed. Or different coloured strips can be used for different types of media, as was suggested with 5in X 3in cards. Confusion can arise if too many colours are used. Or you may find you have decided to try to distinguish too many groups and have run out of available colours! Limit your groups to about half a dozen.

Organization and use of the library/resource centre

Cataloguing

To watch any serious quiz game on television is to watch a very impressive demonstration of the potential of the human mind, with its instant recall and enormous memory bank. However, in any library it is very unwise to rely on this aid. At this moment many school libraries are functioning well because someone has a detailed knowledge of the stock and, after a moment's thought, can produce what is required, even if it is contained within a wider subject. For instance, there could be an excellent chapter on volcanoes in a book on South America and another in a book on geology – such a person would know about these. One is reminded in this context of a specialist library which gave a wonderful service, until the man in charge was killed in a road accident and his successor was nearly driven mad by her inability to satisfy inquiries. Such tragic situations are fortunately rare but people come and people go, taking their memories with them. Teachers often leave a school, taking with them a wealth of knowledge about people, places, organizations that they have found invaluable. A useful way of extracting this from them and preserving it for posterity is to devise index cards with short headed sections such as *who, what* or *where it is. Purpose. Other information.* Space should be left for a subject heading by which it can be filed, this being added by the resource organizer.

Before describing how to catalogue your library, in fact how to evolve a way of finding the information you need, mention must be made of a kind of numbering common in schools, but which has no direct bearing on the subject content of an item. These numbers are called accession numbers and some authorities demand their use for auditing. An accession number is a running number given to an item when it is added to stock. Each copy of a book has its own number, which is a help in identifying a book, particularly when one is lost, or when a child returns the wrong copy, leaving another child worried that he has lost a book. An 'accession register' is frowned upon by many experts, but it still has its use in a primary school. It need not be anything grand (a foolscap notebook will do) but, as will be explained later, it can provide a handy record of all the particulars of a book and save a great deal of labour in writing catalogue cards. A typical page of an accession register could look like this:

Acc No	Author	Title	Publisher	Price	Class No
86/1	Cresswell	Bagthorpes Haunted	Faber	£7.95	F
86/2	Barrett	Space Shuttle	Watts	£4.50	629
86/3	Clay	Animals in your Home	Black	£2.50	590
86/4	Iveson	Your Eyes	Wayland	£3.50	612
86/5	Kingsley	The Water Babies	Puffin	£1.50	F
86/6	Scott	The Magic Horse	MacRae	£5.95	F

Figure 15. A typical page of an accession register

The prefix 86 indicates that the book was added to stock in 1986. A more usual method is to number from 0 to the last number given to the most recent book received. You could also provide a column for the International Standard Book Number.

Provided the accession number is quoted on the catalogue cards, a minimum of information is needed on each card (the details are in the accession register). When a book is discarded the entry is deleted at the same time as the catalogue cards are removed. It is not advisable to 'use up' old numbers. Before now books considered irretrievably lost have turned up, causing confusion by duplication of identity numbers.

Some schools have a separate run of accession numbers for each medium. When the numbers appear on catalogue cards in a multi-media catalogue each number is prefixed by a medium designator, eg, F/S 120 or 120 F/S is filmstrip 120, the filmstrips being arranged in numerical order. This is not the same as allocating blocks of numbers to each medium. Each medium has a running sequence of its own and the newest item has the highest number. If the items are arranged in numerical order and the number appears on the record card, care must be taken that no one confuses these numbers with Dewey numbers. One way to avoid this is to have coloured cards for non-book materials and to indicate the Dewey number at the top of the card and the running number and medium designation at the bottom. But this kind of refinement is best avoided. In the end the closest integration into the main system is the best policy for information retrieval.

The usual way of retrieving information is via a subject index and some kind of library catalogue.

The key to the whole system of information retrieval is of course the subject index. It would be quite possible to run a primary school library with only a carefully compiled subject index and no catalogue at all. A subject index should be the key to the catalogue, the books on the shelves and to the audio-visual materials. In fact, a classified catalogue without a subject index is only a shelf list, as the cards are arranged in the same order as the books on the shelves. And a collection of books without a subject index means an inquirer must wander aimlessly round the shelves looking for the right section.

What many people regard as a conventional library catalogue consists of 5in × 3in cards arranged in at least two separate sequences, ideally in four, because fiction and non-fiction require separate catalogues. This needs to be said because the word 'catalogue' conjures up different images in people's minds. One has spoken to groups of teachers about a 'catalogue' and suddenly been aware that some were thinking about seeds and others of mail orders.

The four sequences are: non-fiction in classified (subject) order, non-fiction in author order, fiction in author order and fiction in title order.

If you decide you cannot manage a full-sized catalogue it is perfectly reasonable to omit the author catalogue for non-fiction. It can be assumed that an inquirer wanting a particular item knows why he wants it (eg, it is a very good book on otters) so it will not be difficult to find in the appropriate subject section. Fiction books are probably quite adequately recorded under title only, but this may present problems with the inquirer who wants to know about other story books by the same author when at that particular moment they are all 'out'.

For an information book two identical cards are needed. One will be filed in alphabetical order by the author's name and one by the Dewey number. Several cards with the same Dewey number are filed in alphabetical order by the author's name in their own small sequence.

```
                                    380
        Moore, Michael
          Container ship
          Hamish Hamilton 1985
```

Figure 16.

You can, of course add more details, eg, price, number of pages or an annotation.

Or, if you use accession numbers and have an accession register, you can omit everything except Dewey number, author and title and add the accession number to the card. The bottom left-hand corner is the best place for this number (it is then not likely to be confused with a Dewey number). Should you require

90

further details about the book, to replace it or buy another copy you can quickly find them in the accession register.

Should an information book deal with more than one subject, a decision must be taken as to where to put the book, at the same time drawing attention in the classified catalogue to the secondary subject. A book on training horses for Western films could be shelved at 636, among the other horse books, but the catalogue card in the classified catalogue would give the Dewey numbers thus:

636   (for horses)
(791)   (for films)

and a second card or 'added entry' would be filed

(791)
636

the brackets indicating the subject content but not the shelf location.

Fiction books require two cards set out differently. For the author sequence:

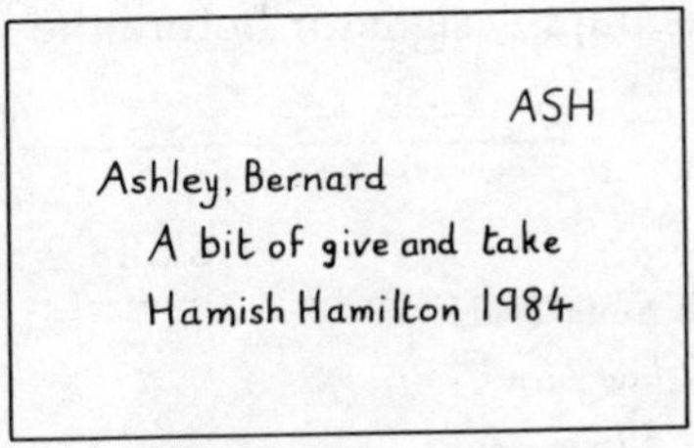

Figure 17.

For the title sequence see Figure 18.

The same decision about how much detail to add applies whether the book is fiction or non-fiction. If you have an author catalogue for non-fiction, cards describing non-book materials do present problems of filing, since there is often no

```
                    ASH
        A bit of give and take
            by Bernard Ashley
          Hamish Hamilton 1984
```

Figure 18.

obvious author. The easiest thing is to give each such item one
card only and file this in the correct sequence in the classified (subject) catalogue using the first word of the title as the
key word. Some items may need a second card in a second
subject sequence, an 'added entry'.

You should indicate that the item is not a book. Some discussion on
this has been included in the section on colour coding. However,
it is perfectly easy to indicate the medium without the use of
colour. A simple letter code to cover all media is given in *Cataloguing rules for books and other media*, published by the School
Library Association. But it is not very arduous to write out the
word in full or you could have rubber stamps made, one for each
medium. Put the medium designator before the Dewey number.

```
                              F/S 598.2
          Song birds
          Ladybird
          35mm double fr
          24 fr coloured
          Conventional vertical feed format
```

Figure 19.

You need only give enough descriptive details to identify the
item and to tell the inquirer whether it is suitable for his purpose.

A similar simple entry could be devised for microcomputer discs, using code Md. The organization of microcomputer resources should, in general, follow the same principles as those for books and audio-visual materials; all software must be classified and colour coded or you will waste time looking for things. However, if the collection only comprises a few items, cataloguing may not be necessary — a good subject index and clear lettering on containers should be adequate guides.

Of course, if your schools library service supplies you with books processed, classified and equipped with catalogue cards none of this applies to you. It is already done for you. All you have to do is file the cards in the correct sequences.

There is another form of catalogue, a dictionary catalogue, which combines all the sequences just described into one long sequence. It also attempts to tackle the problem of indexing the content of a multi-subject resource. It has its devotees but cannot be recommended here where we are dealing with the organization of resources in a primary school.

To take an extreme example, a book called *Houses, food and clothes in Ancient China* could be given cards headed 'Houses', 'Food', 'Clothes' and 'China — ancient history', but each card will bear the Dewey number 931 indicating that that is where the item is shelved, 931 being the number for Ancient China.

The disadvantage of such a catalogue is that it becomes intimidatingly bulky — so many cards to wade through. Alphabetical order is also very tricky as there is endless confusion between the different types of entry: eg, 'Snow' might be an author, the subject of a biography, the title of a book, or the subject entry! (Using different coloured cards for each type of entry increases the complexity for the compiler and may not help the user very much.) All in all, a dictionary catalogue requires much skill both to compile and to use effectively.

The range of information contained in the dictionary catalogue can be more effectively provided for by filing the same card in separate alphabetical runs: one for the authors, one (if desired) for the title, and one containing cards for individual items of information, filed alphabetically under subject headings (as in the case of the book on China used as an example). This brings us nearly, but not quite, back to the typical conventional catalogue already described – the classified catalogue in Dewey order being replaced by an alphabetical one under subject headings. Added entries of the kind illustrated by the China example are equally possible under either system. (See examples of two Dewey numbers needed for the same item.)

Topic indexes

The problem of locating related information contained in an item classified by its main subject and other problems highlighted by the separation of media, can to some extent be solved by maintaining a topic index. If materials are catalogued, classified and arranged conventionally by Dewey numbers, how can a teacher present a topic which cuts right across the normal subject divisions? Obvious examples are such abstract ideas as 'disaster', 'fear' or 'rescue'. But even a simple subject like 'birds' can be seen to demand varied materials: a short list could include: books about birds, both information books and stories, poems about birds, legendary birds, slides of species, film loops and bird flight, overhead projector transparency of skeleton structure, cassette of bird songs.

Initially someone must collect all the materials together. After they have been used once it is of course possible to retain everything in one large box and issue it as a complete study kit. But this implies tying up a lot of valuable material in one context. It is worth noting that fiction books should not be forgotten when collecting materials – their separation from non-fiction books should not make us lose sight of the valuable information buried in many stories. If therefore it is not practical to keep these materials together everyone can co-operate in maintaining a topic index. Each card in the index (and they need to be large cards) is headed with the name of a topic and filed in alphabetical order. So our card headed 'Birds' lists (possibly with some comments) all the items used by one particular teacher. Others can use this list to retrieve what they want and, it is hoped, will add their own contributions. When any item is withdrawn from stock it is very important to remember to alter the topic index as well as other records.

This cross subject approach is ideally served by a microcomputer. To explain very simply: first fill in a data collection sheet with relevant details of source material. These will include format, date and reading age (if a book). Keywords must be chosen to cover all reasonable demands. These details will be added to a microcomputer disc on which each entry has a running number. Now, provided an acceptable keyword is used, your computer will tell you what is available in your library on your chosen topic. Adding to, or deleting from, this database is of course a simple matter. Most primary schools may not be in a position now, or in the immediate future, to create such a mini database but they will be one day. Looking further ahead, one can see the possibilities of establishing a computer link between the primary and the local comprehensive school, allowing the former access to the latter's database and giving pupils practice in information retrieval.

OCCI (Optical Coincidence Coordinate Indexing) is a printed system devised for industrial and special libraries and some school and college libraries welcomed it with enthusiasm. However, it is not within the scope of most primary schools to undertake such an elaborate system and the stationery involved is expensive. It is not appropriate to describe this system in any detail here; a lucid description with pros and cons can be found in Schools Council Working Paper 43. OCCI provides a 'way in' to complex subjects and could be described as a beginner's guide to key word research. It depends entirely on a 'features list' — a list of subjects, places and historical times. This list must be skilfully compiled and cannot be radically altered once the system is in use. Again, surely done better by a microcomputer if available.

One school has evolved a modified OCCI which seems to work satisfactorily. It is only used for non-book resources. A long alphabetical features list has been compiled from which a teacher chooses the exact word or synonym for what he wants. The long list includes positive concepts such as 'castles' as well as abstract ones such as 'temptation'! Having decided on a suitable term the teacher then finds the matching feature card and withdraws it from the feature card filing cabinet. On this card is a list of numbers. These numbers have been allotted to single items in a quite arbitrary way. They are not Dewey numbers. Blocks of numbers called access numbers, between 000 and 6499, have been allocated to different media. To take three examples at random: numbers 1000 to 1499 are pictures, numbers 3200 to 3499 tapes and (significantly) numbers 5701 to 6499 refer to items within kits (whole kits have numbers 5501 to 5700).

The teacher makes a note of the numbers on the feature card he has selected and then refers to an index on small cards, each card being numbered and filed in numerical order. These cards provide more details of the item (which is stored by its numbers) — these include a description and also a note as to the age level for which it is appropriate. Items are stored in media groups in numerical order, so it is a simple matter to retrieve what is wanted.

This organization cuts right across conventional ideas of library arrangement and includes some of the advantages of OCCI, without its main disadvantage. This features list can be added to, or subtracted from, in a way that is not easy with an OCCI features list, which is linked to a punch card system. It is of course not ideal to have one system for software and another for books, as this school does. The books are classified by Dewey so an inquirer is obliged to consider two different procedures for information retrieval. However, as books and media are stored in closely linked areas, this does not seem to be a serious problem.

Another school has evolved a system which combines subject index, topic index and classified catalogue all in one sequence which includes all media! A rubber stamp 5in X 2in has been made and this is stamped on one side of a larger card:

Volcanoes			
Books	////	Files	////
Slides		Work cards	
Audio cassettes		Floppy disc	////
Video cassettes	////		

Figure 20.

Such a card has a topic heading (eg Volcanoes) and the diagram above indicates that there are books, videos, files and a microcomputer floppy disc available on the subject because small squares next to these media are coloured in with the colour of the *subject*. The choice of media for this example is purely arbitrary, you can record as many types as you have spaces. On the back of the card are listed details of what is available. This ingenious scheme has the advantage that an item can be listed under several subject headings. Fiction books can, and should, be included.

This is a subject-based variation of a system based on what are called 'Uniterm cards'. Using Uniterm cards is an accepted way of collecting information for topics and of 'breaking into' multi-topic books. The system can be used to include material in magazines, separate illustrations, postcards, pamphlets, etc. Each item is given an accession number and unless all the items are housed in one sequence (which is unlikely) you will need an accession file of cards arranged in accession order.

The inquirer first looks up a subject on a card which is headed with both a Dewey number and a subject heading. The accession numbers relating to all the items about a particular subject are listed on this card. Reference from the subject-based card to the numbered card in the accession file will give the inquirer a description and the location of what he wants. The details are on the card in the accession number file. The subject card has only a list of numbers.

This is a brief, inadequate description, of necessity, but should you wish to consider this system you are referred to Sheila Ray's article 'Indexing resources in the primary school' contained in *Not by books alone* published by the School Library Association. The whole article goes into the subject of cataloguing and indexing in great detail and is lucid and helpful. The section on Uniterm cards is only a part of the article but is quoted here as relevant to the problem of topic indexing.

If all these procedures seem very elaborate and too heavy for your present situation, take heed. Some *ad hoc* arrangement may work for a small collection, but as the stock increases so will the muddle. It is quite reasonable to expect a library resource centre to grow with the needs of the school. Many people cannot even remember how theirs began, 'it just grew like Topsy' is frequently the reply given to the question 'How did you start?' But this won't do in the long run. Storage and retrieval systems which cope perfectly well with small collections can collapse under the weight of large ones. The school which says 'we have only 20 filmstrips, it is not worth bothering to index them' should stop and think now. Now the job is small and simple, so lay the foundations of a system with one eye on the future, and when you have 200 filmstrips you can still find what you want.

Arrangement of fiction
Except for with the very young, fiction should be arranged on the shelves in alphabetical order of authors' names. The first letter of the author's surname printed on the spine of the book is enough for a small stock. But if your stock runs into several bays of shelving it is advisable to put the first three letters of the author's name on the spine, to simplify finding books by a particular author.

This is not only the conventional way of arranging fiction, and therefore a help to children using other libraries but it also encourages a child who has found an author he particularly appreciated and would like to read 'another one like that'.

It is unwise to attempt to classify fiction books as though they were information books. They should not be shelved with information books however clearly related to a particular subject, unless it is quite clear that they are story books. Attention can be drawn to books on particular themes by what librarians call 'displays'.

A small collection of books on popular themes (like 'horse stories', 'mystery stories', 'sea stories' or 'war stories') can be set up on a table or on some spare shelves and left there for a couple of weeks or so.

When the display is dismantled the books can be listed under fiction topic headings, either on large cards to take to the shelves or on lists on the wall. Cards (covered with Takibak or similar) are popular with children who feel businesslike carrying them round the shelves and looking for what they want.

Fiction should of course be included in any topic list used for learning. For instance Cynthia Harnett's *A Load of Unicorn* has a vast amount of information about Caxton and early printing; and there are countless other examples.

Many people take fairy stories out of the main fiction sequence and have a special area labelled 'fairy stories'. This should not include myths and legends related to religions and cultures, but is a good way of drawing attention to the numerous collections of fairy tales, ancient and modern, that are available.

It is a very good idea to separate all collections of short stories, especially anthologies by several authors. Many children enjoy short stories and all teachers will be grateful for a system which enables them to find something quickly to read to a class last thing on a wet Friday afternoon.

Many children, not very sure of their reading ability, feel secure enough to try another book in a series they know. One school has little emblems (antelopes, gazelles, etc) on the shelves and keeps the series together to help children in their choice. However, as the books are all by different authors, it might be a better idea to do this occasionally as another type of display.

In some primary schools 'follow-on reading books' are colour coded to indicate reading age. This is a sensible convenient arrangement and the books are sometimes in the classroom and sometimes in a 'reading centre'. In practice it means that a child can be sent to choose for himself a book with a yellow label which he knows is the colour appropriate to his ability. He knows he will find a selection of books which he can read and has the undeniable pleasure of choosing his own book.

Somehow we have to be very careful that this does not cause confusion with colour coding for subject content. We cannot have books in the library colour coded for grades of difficulty *and* for subject content. We must avoid any chance of Fred, who has reached the level of 'red books' in his reading progress, finding himself in the library looking at books with red labels which are all about history and famous people and quite beyond his reading capacity.

One way round this problem is to have different shaped labels for each coding, perhaps stars or triangles to indicate reading ages and small squares on information books. This is not very satisfactory and does need constant reminders and explanations.

Even if the graded reading books are shelved separately and clearly labelled many children will still get confused.

It is probably best not to have shelves of books coded by reading age anywhere in the library/resource centre. If the reading centre is quite separate from the library, preferably in another room in another part of the building, children have no trouble in distinguishing between the significance of the two sets of colours. But there is still a risk of confusion in the classroom.

100

Colour coding by reading age can also be done in topic boxes. These boxes will include fiction and can be issued for use with mixed ability classes and means that there will be something on the chosen topic suited to each child's reading age and ability.

Six copies of a selected paperback can be stored in a pamphlet box coded by reading age and a teacher choosing four or more boxes can be almost sure of finding something for everyone to read. Duplication of titles in this way saves many an argument over a popular book.

There are many devices to encourage children to read stories, this is not the appropriate place to discuss them. But it must be said that there is no substitute for an enthusiastic teacher who reads and recommends stories.

Keeping track
The need for a system which provides a way of tracking down specific information is obvious. What is not always so obvious, until the system breaks down, is the need to track down an individual item. There are two specific reasons for wanting to do this. One is a request for an item known to be in stock. Your indexing and cataloguing system should cope with this.

The other reason is that a teacher may ask for an item to be added to stock because it has been recommended, he has used it before, or he saw it in a bookshop or exhibition. Children often ask for books they have seen or stories they have heard. The coordinator should be able to trace how far the book has gone down the 'pipeline' (to answer impatient queries) and inform the inquirer when the book arrives. A system will be described based on books, but it takes only a little ingenuity to apply it to software. It may not be appropriate to all ways of working, but it is useful and simple. You require only lined 5in X 3in cards, rubber bands and a box to take several bundles of cards. The information on each card *must* be uniformly laid out and it is wise to devise a master card, along these lines:

Author		Dewey no
Title		
Date	Publisher	Price
ISBN	Invoice no	Date ord
Received	Acc no	Withdrawn
Remarks		

Figure 21.

The same card will be used for the book from the moment it is suggested until it is finally withdrawn. The box containing cards should be kept securely hidden and labelled 'Items in progress'.

Now to go through the routine step by step.

Stage 1
Miss Smith asks you to order a particular book. Fill in on a card all known details, probably only author and title. Put this card in a rubber band, with others at the same stage, and label the bundle 'Suggested for ordering'. Write on the bottom line of the card the name of the person who suggested the book, or any other details of interest, such as reading or interest age.

Stage 2
Whenever time allows, fill in details which are required before the book can be ordered, eg publisher, price and ISBN. ISBN stands for International Standard Book Number and some authorities will not accept an order from a school without this number. The Standard Book Numbering scheme began to operate in the autumn of 1967. The growth in size and complexity of the book trade imposed an increasing use of computers on publishers, booksellers and wholesalers. A book title has to be translated into a number before a computer can function in the book trade. This number is actually a code, containing all the essential details which are thus stored in the computer file. The numbers are unique and nonchangeable, and they are allocated

according to a standard system adopted originally by the whole
of the British book world. At first there were only nine digits
in each number, but when the idea became international, it was
decided to add one more digit to indicate the country of origin.
Each country has its own code number, on the same principle as
STD dialling codes. British ISBN numbers are nine digits preceded
by 0.

Unless you are compelled to put these numbers on your order
forms, ignore them. Finding an ISBN can be very time consum-
ing. Once all the details required for ordering are completed,
put the card into another bundle labelled 'Ready for ordering'.
When this bundle contains a number of cards, it is time to write
out the requisition form. Of course, the cards will include not
only 'special requests', but also details of books the coordinator
has decided to buy. This is a lot less trouble than conjuring up a
requisition at the end of term, or when one is told there is
some money available. It cuts out endless searching through
publishers' catalogues and should be kept as an ongoing thing.

Stage 3
Fill in the date ordered and invoice number, then file cards in a
bundle or drawer labelled 'Books ordered'.

Stage 4
When the item is received, complete the card in every detail,
except for the withdrawn date. Fiction will have the first three
letters of the author's surname in the right-hand corner, not a
Dewey number. It is important to fill in the date of publication
of non-fiction books. This is always in the book, but may not
have been known to you when you ordered it. Now you have
seen the book, you may wish to add some further annotation or
comment on the bottom line. In the case of fiction, you may wish
to indicate the type of story, or there may be some detail about
an information book you can add, now you have seen it.

You are now left with a card looking something like
Figure 22.

BOOVER, Michael		599
The life of strange mammals		
1975	Macdonald	£1.50
0 356 050971	4328	21.4.86
10.5.86	834	
Requested by Miss Smith Good illustrations		

Figure 22.

Inform the inquirer that the item requested has been received and reserve the item to be collected. Other items can be shelved. File cards in any way you wish, by author, by Dewey number or by title. An 'instant' catalogue, in fact.

You are also left with a collection of cards for books which have not arrived. These need checking regularly, they need not be filed separately, just check the date of ordering from time to time and try to find out why the book has not been delivered.

When a book is finally discarded, withdraw its card and destroy it. If you wish to replace the book copy details on to a new card and use for re-ordering.

Loan systems
The need to keep track of individual items, as well as to retrieve information, soon highlights the need for an efficient loan system. Unfortunately, some of the simplest systems are very vulnerable and any routine based on trust ('help yourself and bring it back at the end of the day') is almost certainly doomed to failure — although there are schools who declare they have no problems and lose next to nothing.

Your loan system will be largely conditioned by the general organization of your library resource centre and by the size and structure of your school. No one system is actually 'better' than any other, but systems based on signing names, or writing out titles,

104

do have grave disadvantages. In this section, we will concentrate on loans of books and software. Hardware centralization and borrowing procedures are discussed elsewhere.

For records of loans from a classroom library, a notebook ruled in columns is probably adequate.

Issued	Borrower	Author	Title	Returned
1.4.86	Sandra King	Kemp	The Clock Tower Ghost	2.5.86
1.4.86	Fred Smith	Ladybird	Book of Cars	7.5.86
2.4.86	George Wilson	Bron/Frank	Amazing Trains	21.5.86

Such a record must be maintained by the teacher or a responsible child, and is not adequate for a centralized collection. There are endless reasons why people do not enter items in a notebook: they forget, they have nothing to write with, someone has picked up the book and put it down in the wrong place, etc.

A development of the notebook system is to have a notebook for each class in the library/resource centre. The pages are in alphabetical order of the children's names and an adult in charge writes down what each child borrows, thus building up a record of what each child has read for the class teacher's convenience.

In one school, children are only allowed to take books home at weekends and a mother comes in every Friday and records what each child borrows (this also is a way of keeping an eye on what each child is reading and making sure that they are all at least borrowing a book).

Any system which faces the user with the vagaries of individual handwriting and varying degrees of illegibility is handicapped. The more mechanical and simple processes of recording loans may demand more initial organization, but they do reduce the chance of loans not being recorded and facilitate the return and shelving of large numbers of items.

Another system, which also involves writing, seems to survive in many primary schools. It involves having either an individual card (about 80mm X 70mm) for each book, or a similar card for each borrower.

If there is an individual card for each book it will be kept inside a pocket, pasted in the book, while the book is on the shelves. On the top of the card will be written the author's name, title of the book and some number or code to identify which copy is on loan. Where there is more than one copy of a book it is essential to distinguish them. This is one advantage of giving every item a running number (accession number) when it is added to stock.

When the book is borrowed, the child's name is written on the card and the cards are filed either in numerical or alphabetical order. The cards can be in one long sequence or in groups behind a date or class teacher's name. If the cards are filed in alphabetical order, it is a simple matter to trace a book, or any other item if the system is used for all media.

Having an individual card for each borrower is not so practical and the cards should really be kept and entered up by a teacher. They do provide some record of what each child has read, or at least borrowed, but they make tracing individual items tedious.

Before the advent of photochanging and electric pens, everyone who used a public library was familiar with the loan system that involved one or more pocket-like tickets for each borrower and a small card for each book. The book card is kept in a pocket pasted inside the book and when the book is borrowed, the card is transferred to the reader's ticket.

How records are to be filed, and where they are to be kept, needs some thought. If children are given individual tickets, they should not be asked to look after them when they have no book on loan. Tickets will get lost or will be illicitly used by other children. The tickets and bookcards linked together are probably best filed in alphabetical order of children's names. They can be kept in the classroom, but for the general purposes, it is practical to file them in the library in one tray in groups behind a marker giving the class teacher's name or identity number of each class. This encourages children to return their books to the centre and means that the searcher for an individual item known to be on loan has only one place to look. If reader's ticket pockets remain permanently in the file, empty tickets are an indication of children who have not borrowed a book. It is better not to issue young children with more than one ticket pocket. If they borrow more than one book, insert book cards together into ticket pocket. Then if they return only one book on some occasion, they can be reminded that they have another. Conversely, an empty ticket can be a comfort to an anxious child who thinks he has lost a book but has, in fact, not borrowed one.

If preferred each class can have a small box (clearly labelled with teacher's name or class identity number) and containing all the readers' tickets and the cards of books on loan. These can be kept on a special shelf in the library but can be taken into the classroom for checking from time to time. Public library loan systems are based on due dates for return and filed accordingly, but this is not very sensible in a primary school. It is better to file records according to class or room number or teacher's name. The length of time children take to read a book varies enormously and it is quite reasonable to allow them to keep an item for as long as they require it (provided of course no one else is waiting for it and it is returned at the end of term). Instead of keeping individual's tickets in a file they can be posted, or clipped, on to hessian or card and hung up in the classroom. The teacher can then easily see who has books out and gathering books in at the end of term is simplified. One school hangs a hessian strip, with attached tickets, outside each classroom door so that anyone looking for a particular item can check whether it is on loan to that class. One can only admire the standard of discipline required to maintain this system but would hesitate to recommend it to all schools.

Another simple system, dependent also on some degree of trust and on the quality of relationships in the school, is to make a pocket chart of hessian, wood, or wood and hessian and hang it on the library wall. There is a pocket for each class and into it go bookcards, individually or in bundles in the case of bulk loans. Borrowers' names are not bothered about, the teacher just asking 'who has this?'.

A similar system called a 'library wall chart' which consists of cardboard pockets (bearing the children's names) pasted on board is often used in classrooms. This way the teacher can see at a glance who has not got a book on loan. In secondary schools, pupils should be required to take responsibility for books they borrow, but in infant and junior schools, the teacher needs to be aware of what is being borrowed, even if the choice of material and the ultimate responsibility for returning it is the child's. Teachers' loans need a slightly different approach because they are likely to borrow books in quantity. More than 5 or 6 cards need to be filed in alphabetical or numerical order and one small ticket pocket may well be inadequate to contain a number of book cards. The simplest thing is to tie tickets together with a rubber band with the teacher's name card as card number one. The bundles can then be filed in alphabetical order of teachers' names and loans checked at least once a term by the coordinator.

The system for teachers' loans should be able to accommodate records of topic loans, ie, groups of material relevant to a topic and borrowed for class use. Probably the book cards should be filed (separately labelled) behind the teacher's other loans. These topic loans are likely to be returned *en bloc* and this system may help other teachers to trace some item they want for some related topic. If the school stock includes topic boxes containing materials collected together and permanently kept together, these will be issued as one item and recorded on suitably descriptive cards. But each box must have an index of contents securely pasted on. On its return to the resources centre, the contents should immediately be checked for missing items. The same check is essential for multi-media kits.

Keeping multi-media kits and topic boxes up to date, and re-placing battered items, are only parts of the complex job of stock editing. Perhaps all these precautions seem too much bother, or perhaps you are daunted by the idea of sticking on so many pockets and writing so many cards or by the expense of buying all the stationery. It is, however, generally accepted that, except in very small schools, tightly organized loan systems are essential. The actual labour of sticking in book pockets and writing out simple cards can be done happily by responsible children. It is only a mammoth undertaking if a whole stock has to be done. Once done it is only a matter of processing new books as they arrive. The stationery is not expensive and can be obtained easily and quickly from several library suppliers.

Even if you regard your library/resource centre as a workshop and consider much of your material to be for reference and consultation in the library, even if you discourage loans to classrooms and home loans are only made from classroom collections, still there may be occasions when a book or other item is taken away with special permission. For this contingency you can make large cardboard markers, like book markers. When a book is borrowed the identification number of a class or a teacher's name is written on the marker, which is left in the gap on the shelves. A monitor is responsible for checking round the shelves and making sure that these books are returned, preferably at the end of the school day. Such a check is particularly important when single volumes from sets of encyclopædias are borrowed.

All these issue systems described can be adapted to all media. One has only to stick pockets on to containers, inside or out, instead of inside a book. This survey of issue systems is not definitive. There are many variations in methods used. All that needs be considered is whether the system in your school is simple, practical, understood and used by all borrowers conscientiously. If it causes problems or fails to keep track of items on loan, it needs revising.

Staffing the library/resource centre

For some time now it has been accepted practice to make responsibility for the library the *raison d'être* for a scale post in a primary school. In Scotland this responsibility is given to promoted teachers. Unfortunately neither situation carries with it an automatic allowance of time. Many, too many, library/resource centres depend for their very existence on goodwill. The teacher concerned is happy to attend to the organization and routine after school hours, even in the school holidays, but no enterprise should be dependent on goodwill alone, which may well depart with the party concerned.

One very large metropolitan authority states that its policy is to establish and maintain library facilities in its primary schools. In each school there is an established post of responsibility, which must be given to someone who will take charge of the library. But no recognized allocation of time is quoted from on high. Heads are advised, even urged, to give a teacher time to run a library, but this can vary greatly from school to school. It should be a local education authority responsibility to insist on a recommended amount of time being allocated to running the library in a primary school.

Occasionally, but very rarely, ways are devised to keep a teacher in the library all day. But of course all these arrangements are at the mercy of the exigencies of a school day, absentee teachers, etc. It is a pity that primary school teachers do not have, as secondary school teachers do, an allocation of 'free' periods which could be spent in the library, not working but just giving support by being there.

111

Ironically, but understandably, the vastly increased use of audio-visual aids has made the metropolitan authority referred to above recognize the need for help in primary schools and some appointments have been made to look after resources and create material for teachers. Now a few primary schools have media resource officers of their own, while some, involved in joint resource schemes, share one between them. Book libraries have muddled on for years and not until they are efficiently organized does anyone realize how much they have to contribute. Some authorities have library advisers whose responsibilities also include drama and English, others have library advisers *per se* and one even has a team of advisers, who, with practical awareness of the difficulties involved, do their best to help and advise teachers in charge of primary school libraries. For all these people the task is extremely daunting and would be more rewarding and productive if there were sensible arrangements authorized within the schools.

This section will try to offer some suggestions for running a library/resource centre without spare time or money to pay for help!

In one school the headmaster is in charge of the library resource centre, because he feels resource-based learning is an integral part of the philosophy of the school. Infant resource organization is delegated, so are the creation and exploitation of learning packs. A great deal of continuing maintenance is also delegated, to ensure continuity of policy and to make certain that virtually every teacher is trained in the use of the centre and feels involved. An auxiliary does much of the day-to-day running, under teacher direction, to supply what teachers need.

Another headmaster considers himself more available during the working day than any class teacher. So he is on call at all times, and happy to be the school librarian.

Not all headteachers are so enthusiastic, but many a deputy head is in complete charge of organizing resources, with the obvious advantage that he/she has enough authority to insist on an agreed organization and impose regulations.

Teachers in charge of primary school library/resource centres may interpret the job in different ways, or an interpretation may be forced on them by the school. A teacher with real enthusiasm for, and knowledge of, children's books, sees the promotion and enjoyment of reading as one of the prime aims of a library/resource centre, and so books will take their place with the other media. However, such a person needs to have the backing and help of a technician of some kind and where this can be done a very satisfactory, balanced situation emerges.

One primary school has two teachers closely involved with the library/resource centre. The coordinator has overall responsibility and because the school is semi open-plan and the teaching is team teaching, she can be released for sizeable amounts of time. The other teacher has been on a course on all aspects of resource-based learning and, although a highly creative person, is also prepared, and able, to maintain, repair and 'set up' equipment.

In yet another school the teacher in charge of the library considers herself in charge only of the books. She has no spare time, so has trained the children to run the library on a rota system of monitors. This they do very well. The software is 'administered' by another teacher and is used for teaching only. The non-book material is not cross-referenced with the books, so there is total separation. So long as two people are involved in such a situation this dichotomy will continue. It is a not uncommon situation, often forced on a school because of space. A 'resource centre' separated from the book library tends to become only a support service for teachers, with no child involvement except in the teaching area.

One school acquired an out-of-work teacher, on some job creation scheme. There are many advantages in having such a person in the school. A teacher or librarian will have skills invaluable to the resource centre and will also be qualified to take some responsibilities for looking after the pupils both in school and on outside visits, to the library, museum, etc.

ROPS-H

A clerical assistant is 'resident' in one library/resource centre all day and the science laboratory technician is expected to look after the hardware. This excellent arrangement is about to be cut off because of compulsory cuts in auxiliary staff, which will curtail the use of this centre by 50%. The deputy head is in charge of the centre but he does full-time teaching and his free time is getting less and less.

Some authorities have establishment for clerical or technical assistants, on a recognized grade, who can be asked to help run the library/resource centre. Whoever is appointed should supplement skills already in the school and it is pertinent to consider whether technical help is needed more than clerical, or *vice versa*.

Where full-time non-teaching help is available the person is often based all day in the 'audio resource centre' or 'control centre' and provides a support service for teachers, which will probably include looking after and tending software, recording television and radio programmes and repairing equipment — a support service to teachers which is badly needed.

Assuming that your school has an integrated resource centre equipped to give a good service to both staff and pupils, you are inevitably faced with the problem of how to keep it open all day. Even in the situations already described no one person can be there all the time. Some arrangements must be made within the framework of the school management so that no auxiliary is left at the mercy of the staff or expected to be at everyone's beck and call. The job specification should be clear and duty time clearly defined. Even a full-time coordinator needs some time off, and there is always the knotty problem of lunchtime duties. However part-time hours for non-teaching staff are usually adjustable (but the playground has to be supervised as well as the library).

Some partial solution can be found by timetabling *small* remedial groups in the centre, taught all day by the same teacher. But the groups must be small, or they will prevent other uses of the library, and the teacher must be prepared to put up with the interruptions from individual inquirers who need help. It has been pointed out that this situation is very beneficial to the less able pupils, who are being taught surrounded by books, and who see other pupils using them with enjoyment.

Any teacher who takes a class into the library is of course responsible for them and is thus providing adult supervision. A few individual inquirers from other classes can be dealt with in this situation, but not very satisfactorily. The problem remains that the genuine, interested searcher for knowledge may well be permanently discouraged if it seems to him that he can 'never' get into the library when he wants to.

It is very important to have clear directives to both teachers and pupils about opening times and no pupil should ever be turned away from the library without being told when he *can* come, the sooner the better.

Parents are often enthusiastic about the idea of helping in any kind of library, which they can clearly see is an asset to their children. But one bitter complaint about parental help is that parents sometimes 'carry out proceedings in direct conflict with the instructions they have been given'. This is a common problem with volunteers who then, if criticized, disappear. This is another situation where the job specification should be quite clear, the tasks defined and limits set on what the parents are expected to do.

One school has successfully organized no fewer than 16 parents as aides, (on a rota system) both in the library/resource centre and in the teaching areas. Such a team of course needs careful tactful organization. Other schools talk of 'harnessing' parent help and using it for book jacketing and other tasks. A large team requires to be very firmly organized and prepared for. Work should be ready for them to do, no one should be kept hanging about all afternoon and go home feeling they have wasted their time.

Many simple duties can of course be carried out by children or less academic auxiliaries. Children can easily be trained in all sorts of library duties which seem to appeal to them. Child help

115

is discussed in detail in another section. The more jobs they are given in the library the better they will understand how it functions and the more responsibility they will feel for its welfare. This is all good training but some rota system is needed to ensure that their library duties do not interfere with their education.

All these various forms of help need to be supported by some simple manual of practice so that anyone can take over any task with understanding. Suggestions for a manual of practice are gone into in more detail in the section on in-service training of teachers and training of pupils.

Many jobs only need simple training, but it is not right to depend on the same few people always to do them. School helpers are frequently mentioned as being very helpful in libraries, but which comes first, a child with a badly cut knee or duty time in the library? Things must be arranged so that someone else can always take over.

In-service training of teachers

However simple and logical the arrangement of resources in a primary school, there are bound to be facts of day-to-day practice that need to be explained to new arrivals — staff or pupils — or to a teacher who wants to extend his use of resources to develop a new idea. Teachers must abide by the simple rules of the library/resource centre (and must be seen to do so by the children) so they need to know the rules. For these reasons many schools find it worthwhile to produce quite detailed 'guides' and handouts on the management and use of the resource centre. Some explain the basic principles of the Dewey Classification system and go on from there to explain the retrieval system. Others offer simple guidelines on how to find information and explain what materials are available and explain how loans must be recorded. It is surprising that this is not always done as a matter of course.

One reason may be that newcomers to a school are deluged with paper. A handout, however carefully prepared, may be regarded as just another wad of paper to be ignored.

116

If possible, in addition to a handout, some kind of short induction course should be given to new staff, preferably in the library/resource centre. At the very least it is suggested that early in the new term the headteacher, or library coordinator, could go through the handout with new members of staff. It might then be appreciated and referred to when needed. This could even be done at a staff meeting when comments from other members of staff would be helpful.

It is equally important that a demonstration of the use of more complicated pieces of hardware should be given before anyone uses anything for the first time!

Understanding and manipulating individual pieces of equipment is not something that should be included in general information about organization and routine. Detailed instructions on the use of hardware should be attached to each item, or stored with it. Sad to say very few people actually read instructions, until some breakdown occurs. But it is sensible to have a few clear 'dos and don'ts' attached to any mechanical device used by several people.

The guidelines described above are not the same as a manual of practice for the organization of the library.

A manual of practice should be compiled by the coordinator to be used by his successor or temporary substitute. No one expects to stay in one job for ever and it is vital that there should be continuity. If there are no written instructions utter chaos can follow the departure of a coordinator, or even an absence through illness. The manual need only be a notebook, kept somewhere safe but freely available to anyone who takes over all, or any part of the routine. Step-by-step procedures for ordering, processing, cataloguing and classifying all media need to be recorded.

The necessary routine for keeping track of stock, from its arrival in the school until it is finally discarded, is explained in another section.

Involving the children

If a school library/resource centre is to achieve its full potential the children must be deeply involved. And this is the area where two conflicting demands made on a resource centre become obvious. It needs to be a supporting service for teachers, a time-saving, useful tool. So it is reasonable to supply teachers with made-up multi-media packs based on topics, because it is not reasonable to expect searches for material for similar topics to be done over and over again. Every simple practical short cut is a bonus. However, too great an emphasis on teacher aids can lead to a situation where children are considered 'too careless' to handle equipment or where they are not allowed access to anything but books. This is a pity. Children can be trained to be of invaluable help in the day-to-day running of a library and the more responsibility they have the more care they will take. Also doing individual research, finding out for themselves, in a well-run library/resource centre is an enjoyable, valuable part of education. It is not easy to cater for the different needs of teachers and children, but the best school library/resource centres manage it, and the skills learnt are valuable throughout life.

The cognitive and mechanical skills involved in using library books and other information sources need to be taught consciously, especially as they are so important in the secondary steps of education, particularly for CSE students.

A letter from Martin Wright of the Howard League for Penal Reform headed 'Why don't students do their own digging in libraries' and published in *The Times Educational Supplement* complained (on behalf of all voluntary organizations) of the enormous number of requests for information they receive. He then went on to say 'Few of the inquiries we receive give any indication of an attempt to find information in a library. Wouldn't it be of more use to the children to show them, with the help of a librarian, how much they can find out for themselves, rather than give them the idea that the only way to get information is to discover the right specialist organization and write to it?' There are probably two reasons for the state of affairs. Pupils may not have been trained

118

to exhaust all the resources in the school before going outside for help. Teachers may seize on this kind of opportunity to teach their pupils how to write formal letters, without giving a thought to the recipient.

His plea is echoed by many colleges of education who find it necessary to run simple basic courses for their students before they can use the library at all.

The most enjoyable way for a pupil to learn how to use a library/ resource centre is to be encouraged to focus on some specific interest in which he is already involved. He will be eager to learn how to use the library organization to find out more. But in practice there are many children who do not readily express enthusiasm for any hobby. A school which takes resource-based learning seriously builds the use of the library/resource centre into almost every learning task. We have to avoid the danger of the little specialist seeing the library/resource centre only as a bonus to add to his particular knowledge, and make sure that he sees it in a wider context and also ensure that others begin to realize its potential for them.

No opportunity to show how the system works should ever be missed. It takes more time and patience to show a pupil how to find out the difference between a butterfly and a moth than it does to show him a slide or picture and point out the difference. But the skill involved in simple research will not be forgotten and the pupil has a real sense of achievement each time his search is rewarded.

If too much research done in the library/resource centre is based on workcards the children develop the 'treasure hunt' syndrome and become adept at answering questions without really caring what the answer is. This is not giving them a proper attitude to the library, or any real understanding of research.

Involve pupils in the development of the library/resource centre as well as in its organization. One school which had no visible subject

119

index got the pupils to devise the first list of headings. A class of top juniors were each given three pieces of paper numbered 1, 2 and 3. On number 1 they were asked to write something they knew a lot about, on number 2 something about which they knew little and would like to know more and on number 3 something they knew nothing about and would like to find out about. This exercise led to a surprising amount of useful discussion involving correct terminology, synonyms for the same topic and problems of spelling. At the end of it all the teacher was left with numerous ideas for subject headings all expressed to children's terms and she was able to compile a visible index which is used with enthusiasm.

Some schools involve the pupils in carefully structured induction courses on the use of the library. This is necessary after big changes have been made but perhaps not so valuable where a resource centre is accepted and has gradually developed. In one school, children are shown a series of overhead projector transparencies which explain the principles of alphabetical order and apply these to the subject index and so lead on to a simple explanation of the Dewey system. Encyclopædias, indexes, and other available materials are also explained. However not all children will grasp the practical significance of what they have been taught and many will forget before they have a real chance to practise. The only justification for doing this would be if there had never before been any kind of centralized library in the school and the children were now being introduced to something entirely new to them. Otherwise these courses tend to be too abstract and encourage the children to think of 'library' as a subject — which is something that must be avoided at all costs.

The kind of continuing instruction in a learning situation already described inculcates the right ideas. To stop children asking again and again how to start finding what they want (and many will do this just to gain attention) a very simple flow chart, or set of instructions, can be pinned up in the library and easily referred to. (See Figure 23).

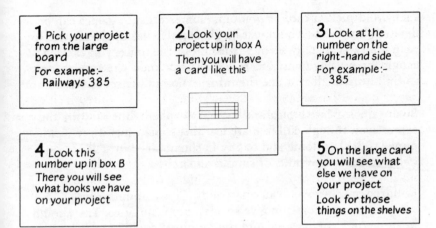

Figure 23. A simple set of instructions to display for easy reference

Another way of reinforcing library instructions is to devise library games, which must not be confused with workcards which relate to a particular topic. To teach the basics of fiction arrangement make twenty or so strips of card (about 20mm X 120mm) and on these write authors' names and ask the children to sort them into alphabetical order. The cards are put out on a table in random order and are to be arranged in progression like rungs of a ladder. At first the children will try to sort these by first names and must be taught to look at surnames. Choose your authors so that children are learning alphabetization up to the third or fourth letter (eg, Todd, Tolkein, Tolstoy, Tomalin, Tomlinson, Townsend). Of course your choice will spread right through the alphabet; the above is an extreme example. Most children find this fun because it involves moving 'rungs' up and down the 'ladder' until the right order is found.

Other games can be devised using 5in X 3in cards. On the cards are simple questions to be answered from an encyclopaedia, or questions relating to Dewey numbers (eg, find books with the number 641, what are they about?) or questions relating to subjects (what is the number/colour for birds? Find a book and set of slides). The cards are handed upside down in a pack to a group of children and each child picks a card at random. Numerous such games can be devised, but the teacher must be absolutely sure of the answer for each query. This may seem a truism, but the unwary have been caught by writing questions to which they knew the answer, only to find it difficult to trace the information in the school resources!

Such games create a pleasant busy atmosphere, but they *are* only games even though children are learning something. They will help pupils to feel at home and happy in the library but will not do much to teach the skills of simple research!

Children are invaluable auxiliary aids. Chosen pupils can be designated monitors and give special responsibilities. This should be done on a rota system and the monitors should feel it is a privilege to be chosen. One school has a clearly written handout for 'librarians' which sets out the library rules, 'Your duties as a librarian', and goes on to explain the basic arrangement of the library, how to use the subject index, and how to issue books. The children look after the book stock, software is managed by a teacher. The teacher in charge of the library has a full teaching timetable and during the day the library is managed solely by children.

Children can easily be trained in all kinds of library duties, which seem to appeal to them. They can be involved in the day-to-day maintenance of the library, tidying up at the end of the day, replacing materials after class visits, etc. It is a good idea to make individual children responsible for keeping one area of the library tidy and encourage some element of competition. Children can also help to process books, after a little initial training. They can use a Dymo marker, stick on pockets and labels or put on plastic jackets. Issuing and taking in borrowed items can also be done by child monitors but this must be undertaken by reliable volunteers with a sense of responsibility as simple errors make for desperate muddles.

No one should have too long on one task or they become bored and careless. Ring the changes and teach them as many skills as possible. Unless of course someone really likes doing a particular

122

job and does it well. This often applies to the less able child who is happy to have found a niche and feel he has a responsibility.

All library duties should be arranged in a rota and there should be a group of chosen children. Too many, and they get bored because there is not enough to do, too few, and their library duties begin to interfere with their education!

The basics of book management are of course equally applicable to software, but when it comes to managing equipment the advantages of child labour have to be weighed against the hazards. Books cannot give electric shocks, nor do they contain delicate mechanisms which can be irrevocably damaged by being dropped. In this electronic age, children very quickly become adept at using equipment, but it is another matter to fetch and carry even small items. Large, heavy equipment should, of course, never be entrusted to them. However, at least one school allocates responsibility for hardware management to a group of older children who work in pairs. Responsibility is spread so that no child spends more than a small amount of his time on his duties. Simple trolleys on castors provide a safe way of moving equipment round the school and the needs of teachers are clearly indicated. The children receive careful instructions in how to handle equipment before they embark on a period of duty. Much of the work is done before school or during break periods and there is no lack of volunteers. Here is an obvious example of the usefulness and importance of creating a right sense of involvement and responsibility.

Some recognition of merit, or reward for good service, is always appreciated. Library badges can be given after a certain length of time and after passing some kind of mini-library exam. These will be proudly worn and will carry authority in the library. But care must be taken not to overlook the less able child who could not pass a library test, but may have slogged away for months at some menial task everyone else found boring. He too needs recognition.

The more involved pupils are in the day-to-day running of the library, the more possessive they feel about it. Once the climate of opinion is set against any kind of 'mucking about' or abuse of the library even chronic troublemakers will think twice about creating a disturbance there.

Support services and sources of materials

The purpose of this section is to outline briefly contacts, places, people and organizations outside school which could help you. You should inquire what services are available and press your authority for those you think you should have.

In many areas there is an obvious lack of coordination which results in what one headmaster described as 'widespread ignorance' of outside resources available to teachers.

Services and personnel vary so widely that it is only possible to indicate what you might expect from your local teachers' centres or schools library service. Perhaps some indication of what others have available may give you the courage to demand more.

Most local education authorities have teams of advisory teachers. One mentioned 3 primary advisers and 36 secondary advisers, many of whom were subject-based, but none of whom had any special knowledge of library organization. They would probably be most useful as sources of information about schools with well organized library/resource centres with whom you could exchange ideas.

Schools library service
A well organized schools library service is the thing to hope for. Many of these print a standard subject index which is issued to schools to encourage uniformity in classification and as a first step to centralized cataloguing, as well as centralized processing. The aim is to match the classification of books in the school

libraries with the books in headquarters so that there is no confusion when books are bought centrally or borrowed as long-term loans.

Most schools library services offer regular advice on the use and significance of the subject index and its application to the day-to-day organization of the school.

Books bought from a central library service usually come jacketed and ticketed and the use of a uniform subject index means that they could also come with ready-made catalogue cards. The lending of multi-media collections is on the increase and of course the same principles of uniform classification apply. Used properly, a schools library service is an invaluable aid but it should not become a prop. Schools should still have freedom to choose some materials outside the system and teachers should try to keep up their own knowledge of what is available, not rely entirely on the advice of the school librarian.

The staff of a school library service will be librarians qualified to give helpful advice to individual schools and many print handouts will be available at the centre or widely distributed. These may be book lists or practical advice, eg, 'Some suggestions for handling media'.

Financial arrangements between schools and school library services vary but there is always considerable financial advantage in buying from the local source.

One authority supplies almost unlimited bulk loans on a long-term basis and charges very low prices for books chosen from central stock and bought for school stock. The books are delivered processed and classified. Any other books have to be bought by the school at full price and must of course be jacketed and pocketed and classified in the school by school staff.

Many schools library services have books on education for loan to teachers and permanent displays of children's books to help teachers choose wisely. These exhibitions are widely found, even in areas where there is no central purchasing system.

Special loans and specially made up topic boxes are often part of the service given by schools library services.

In many rural areas, and some urban ones too, both schools library services and public libraries run book vans which visit schools regularly and from which large loans are chosen on a termly or longer basis. Book buses are now appearing which serve a slightly different function. They visit schools like mini-libraries and children make their individual choices. Some have story-telling upstairs and a lending library on the lower deck.

Teachers' centres

Many teachers' centres offer a wide variety of services, some the same as those offered by a schools library service. Here is a list of possibilities, compiled from many centres visited.

Displays of books, both for children and on education
Displays of hardware and compatible software
Ideas for display work in the school library
A mini resource centre set up as an example of what can be achieved
Multi-media displays, subject based
Loan service of teachers' books
Loan service of all media with advice on use

Services: photocopying, slide making, photocopying of source materials, taping broadcasts on request, video-tape recording on request

Courses: on use of audio-visual aids and on making own material.

One teachers' centre lends multi-media packs for particular projects. The packs are graded in four age groups, are lent for one term and arrive in large, strong boxes. This same centre has an extremely useful index of producers and manufacturers which will eventually have a second sequence, referring from media to the various relevant suppliers.

Courses

Regular courses on all aspects of education are usually a great part of the work done by teachers' centres. Most of them have small libraries and regularly put on special exhibitions of books or equipment. Courses, etc, are usually set up by the inspectorate but occasionally outside agencies are involved. Publishers are glad to show their wares and in one case the manufacturers of storage boxes set up an exhibition, talked about their products and were supported by the local audio-visual adviser. This encouraged some local schools to start reorganizing their materials.

Many teachers' centres offer elementary courses on the organization of school library/resource centres. These are nearly always well attended since some people are just beginning and others are happy to go on learning and exchanging ideas.

In the summer of 1977 the Library Association and the School Library Association agreed upon a new certificate in School Library Studies to replace the Teacher-Librarian Certificate. The new certificate, awarded by individual colleges, is course- rather than examination-based: the individual colleges devise the courses and submit them for validation to a Joint Board, set up to oversee and coordinate the courses throughout the country.

The Scottish Council for Educational Technology and the National Audio-Visual Aids Centre also offer an astonishing amount of information relating to both hardware and software. They are able to give very detailed information about equipment and also names and addresses of suppliers.

Free material

A great deal of free material suitable for project work is available from various sources; there are often advertisements in the educational press. For instance, Brooke Bond Oxo Ltd offers a free loan service to schools from its sound film library. Recommended sources of information about free material include *Treasure Chest for Teachers*, Teachers' Publishing Co, revised 1984; *Goldmines: resources for teachers* by David Brown, Epistemology with BP and Dept of Trade and Industry, 1985; and *Free and Cheap Resources for Schools: a survey and guide* edited by Robert S Mason, Library Association, 1985.

Junior Books Limited offer a valuable service to schools and their catalogues are invaluable as sources of suitable books and other materials, to fill gaps in stock. The lists give interest age and reading age and the information books are arranged by Dewey numbers. For a small extra charge they supply paperbacks and picture books laminated and reinforced. They also offer a full library processing service for large orders from a public library service.

Local sources

Provided someone is prepared to do the organization and secretarial work, regular meetings of teachers from local primary schools provide excellent opportunities for exchange of ideas. Some meet to discuss children's books, others to seek help on problems of organization of their library/resource centres. The teachers' centre is the obvious place to meet but it is a good idea to relate the meetings round schools, as the centre may be more accessible to some people than to others. In one area, such meetings are arranged by the local children's librarian.

Your local branch of the School Library Association will certainly hold meetings where you can meet other teacher/librarians faced with similar problems to yours. Informal meetings for discussions or to listen to a speaker are usually held in schools in the evenings. Often visits are arranged to see school or college libraries of particular interest. Some branches manage to run one-day course/conferences on the organization and management of school library/resource centres. Accommodation for these, especially at weekends, is often difficult to find.

What seems to be needed is a clearing house for ideas, and a place for regular meetings. The news that many authorities are now closing down teachers' centres really is quite appalling and shows a total disregard for their potential.

One interesting service is worth mentioning. Isolated families in

129

the Orkney Islands are supplied with 'home boxes'. These are multi-media collections, on any topic requested, and contain materials of interest to the whole family.

This is giving a service to local residents, but they themselves are a valuable source of information. People who have lived a long time in one place can often be persuaded to talk about the past and their memories may be linked to what 'they heard from their grandparents'. Many children are fascinated by talking to old people, but this exercise should not be overdone. The oldest inhabitant can have his days, and his temper, severely shortened by being pestered by children with cameras and tape recorders.

Other sources of local information about the past are local history and archaeology societies. Sometimes (as in Hackney) there are printing and publishing firms who collect reminiscences, old photographs, etc, and publish them, either as personal accounts, or as detailed accounts of a certain area at some steps in its history. Local history societies will often supply photocopies of documents and manuscripts and are prepared to answer questions and encourage children. The public library will have a record of the addresses of all such societies in your area and may well have an interesting 'local collection' of its own.

Churches are a mine of information and vicars are nearly always ready to help in finding interesting sources. Memorial tablets commemorating local personalities and victims of wars can be linked to history projects and there is a wealth of local history in the churchyard. For example, some children wandering around a churchyard found that numerous young children had died, all within the same year. This interested them and a little research revealed that there had been a cholera epidemic that year and so led to projects on public health.

Everyone speaks highly of museum services: some sell slides, nearly all will lend such things as small stuffed birds and animals, shells, stones, armour pieces (helmets, etc) artefacts and replicas of all kinds. Many have workcards and will go to a great deal of trouble to look after visiting children.

Some have an education officer who will come and work with teachers and children in schools, work with them in the museum and on sites and generally advise. Archives of the simplest kinds can be used by primary schoolchildren and some museums and/or record offices have good photocopying services for schools.

All schools should keep their own records of useful sources of information and local places of interest. Teachers should not keep their discoveries to themselves but should share them. How this can be done simply within the school is explained elsewhere; but people should also be prepared to share discoveries with other schools which could add to the interest and value of the regular local meetings already suggested.

No mention has been made of local booksellers as a support service, simply because they are so few and far between. But if you are lucky enough to have one, he will surely let you browse, even if you can only buy the occasional book. And nearly all booksellers are happy to support a school bookshop. The Schools Bookshop Association exists solely to give you all the help and advice you need to set up a school bookshop.

Public library

The public library has so far received only a passing reference but deserves a separate section, so what your school can expect from involvement with it now follows.

The degree of involvement you have with your public library depends on the local government situation in your area. Where the library and the schools are both financed and supervised by the local education authority the public library supplies the same back up service as is generally expected from a schools library service. But sometimes, as in Inner London, the library is the responsibility of the borough, but the schools belong to the education authority. Usually there is plenty of cooperation from the library but this is necessarily based on goodwill and the librarian's conception of his/her duty to the community. Now and again someone raises the nasty question of finance. Is the library justified in lending large numbers of books to schools when the school should be spending some of its capitation allowance on building up its own library?

In such situations it is reasonable to expect two things from the library. In order of priority they are:

1. encouragement to the children to become members of the public library: to achieve this end most librarians will be happy to receive regular class visits, to run story-telling sessions and good readers' clubs and to come to the school and talk about the library.

2. topic loans of say, 20 to 30 books lent to individual teachers for one term or a matter of weeks (special requests for individual books).

It is not reasonable to expect the borough library to provide large bulk loans for long periods.

Alternatively the public library, financed by the same authority as the school, will naturally cooperate by meeting special requests, by giving bulk loans for long periods on a *per capita* basis and by supplying topic loans for agreed periods of time.

It is very rare to find a library of either category that does not delight in its involvement with schools. Many display children's work and all display a close personal interest in their clients and often know more about a particular child's reading tastes than either his teacher or parent.

The librarian should keep close links with the headteacher and any outbreaks of bad behaviour or vandalism should be reported at once. Teachers can also help in recovering overdue books if they are given names of offenders from the librarian.

Any contact with the public library is to be encouraged. Children come to realize that all libraries are arranged on the same basic principles, that they can apply what they have learnt in their school library to finding what they want in a much larger library. They will learn that libraries are linked, nationally and internationally, and come to see that the school library is not something they will leave behind them as they grow up but the beginning of what can become of lifelong help and interest.

Finance

This section can only be brief and general and will consider expenditure on resources needed for the library/resource centre in a school committed to resource-based learning, however organized. It will not include discussion of expenditure or allocation of what is usually called 'stock' – chalk, pencils, paper, rubbers, etc.

Local education authorities' policies on school finances vary widely, and you will already know what is the policy in your own area; so in this section we shall consider a few possibilities and then concentrate on finance within the school.

Initial budgeting for library provision in a new school is done by the local authority and is based on various factors and expectations. Additional furniture, as the library/resource centre expands, will most likely be paid for by the authority. It is not usual for schools to pay for large, expensive items from their own funds. It has long been accepted that the provision of books to form a school's *basic* stock may be treated as capital expenditure and a special grant may be obtained for a library that has been grossly neglected or has never reached a reasonable standard. Sometimes this can be done on the appointment of a new head!

Some authorities allocate a separate library capitation which must be spent on library materials, but even the spending of this must involve joint decisions: decisions depending largely on the way the resources are organized and how many people are actually involved in spending the money. Other authorities make a total capitation allowance and let headteachers spend the money how they wish.

135

There are many varied ways of buying books within different regions: special discounts, decentralized purchasing, etc; and these variations make it difficult to advise on budgeting.

In a primary school the problem of dividing up the money may not be so acute as in a secondary school, where teachers are accustomed to have their own departmental allowance. But many primary schoolteachers may also be used to having their own separate sum of money to spend on classroom provision. The decision to centralize, or reorganize, resources may mean that everyone will have to accept a little less in order to contribute to the central pool.

In practice, the teacher, and above all the library/resource centre coordinator, should have some influence over the allocation and the head may well delegate the division of expenditure in this area to the coordinator.

Figures for recommended expenditure on books are becoming more and more meaningless as prices rise. The ILEA no longer recommends a 'library element' in the capitation for a school year as it once did. The figures from the National Book League for 1985/6 for primary school library books are, per pupil per annum: 'good' £4.75, 'reasonable' £3.95. There are separate figures for class books.

At one stage, in the 1970's the Library Association urged an 'adequate' initial capital grant for furniture and stock. It was recommended that the initial grant should be spent over a number of years in order to cover adequately the needs of the developing school's image and phase the work involved in the building up of the stock. The cost of the initial stock must be related to the current average cost of books and other materials. So far, no-one has suggested how much per capita should be spent on software but obviously provision must be made.

If you are allocated a specific sum, remember that you need stationery (book pockets, ticket labels, etc, etc) and that rubber stamps wear out and subject indexes get tatty. Many school librarians are not in favour of rebinding and make no financial allowance for this. Primary school books are often not worth rebinding because the pages are as worn and dirty as the covers. However, in these days of short print runs and the demise of many a useful book, this is a matter for personal decision. If your library/ resource centre includes a production unit, make sure it is clearly understood who pays for the raw materials. Do not forget to allow for replacing lost and damaged books. Many public libraries find that they need to replace the whole of their juvenile stock in the course of five years.

The chore of processing and indexing new materials is much reduced if you can manage to send in small orders at intervals. This keeps the library constantly renewed and there will be continuing interest among pupils and staff in the new additions. A method of keeping up a system for ordering is explained in the section 'Keeping track'.

Buying library books once a year is attractive in times of acute inflation, but projection of needs is tricky and one may lose the chance of buying useful books published during the year and which may be out of print before the next buying spree. Also the sight of all those books to be processed is daunting and reduces the pleasure of receiving new stock!

The head may be unwilling to promise a positive annual sum and may prefer to keep an eye on the flow of expenditure throughout the year. He may, without warning, inform the coordinator that some money is available and can now be spent on the library. This makes budgeting for the library/resource centre very difficult: an agreed sum for the whole year is a much more sensible arrangement.

In a happier way, unexpected sums of money may come to the coordinator for the library/resource centre. Church schools often mention the generosity of their managers in contributing towards particular items, or for improvements. Money raised by PTA functions may be expressly given to help the library/resource centre, especially if it is expanding and obviously providing a lively, useful service to the school. It is often a good idea to buy something specific with this money, like a new set of encyclopaedias or some interesting piece of equipment.

Try always to keep some money in hand for the entirely unexpected, or for the enthusiastic teacher who suddenly has a bright idea which needs extra financial backing. But, unless your local authority allows money unspent to be carried over into the next financial year, do not be too frugal or you may lose what you have not spent.

On the other hand, the present low turnover besetting publishers can cause a high proportion of books to be temporarily or permanently out of print. This can mean many orders remain unfulfilled and the money which should have been spent is forfeited, unless your authority allows it to be carried over into the following year.

This makes balancing the budget difficult. It is probably safe to order a percentage over the amount one intends to spend each year, but do not overdo it. Some authorities automatically cancel all orders not fulfilled after a certain period (remember to check this in your 'on order' file), others leave the order standing. The sudden arrival of temporarily out-of-print books and their invoices can come as a shock if a school is spent-up.

In the final analysis it is the headteacher's responsibility to ensure that a reasonable proportion of the capitation is allocated for the purchase of resources such as library books, audio-visual software (including film and magnetic tapes and discs for making software), paper, stencils and inks, etc, for making non-book print materials and replacement parts and maintenance charges for equipment; and each headteacher will develop expertise in this complex matter gradually as the library/resource centre becomes established and proves its worth in the school.

A select bibliography

A great deal has been written about library/resource centres over the last few years, recently supplemented by many books and pamphlets about the use of microcomputers. However, much of this is directed at the professional librarian, is applicable only to a large secondary school and needs time and expertise to implement.

This list is only a small selection but includes books personally recommended in various schools as valuable aids to organizing thoughts towards resource-based learning. Most teachers' centres and support services compile bibliographies. These are worth studying, especially as the books should be available to you.

Adapting Spaces for Resource-Based Learning (Guidelines 8) by Barbara Atherton. Council for Educational Technology, 1980.
Audio Cassettes: a guide to selection and management (SLA Guidelines No 2) by Michael Greenhalgh. School Library Association, 1982.
Cataloguing Rules for Books and Other Media in Primary and Secondary Schools by Norman Furlong and Peter Platt. School Library Association, 1984.
Children, Computers and the Curriculum by J J Wellington. Harper and Row, 1985. General introduction to the possible uses of computers in schools. Asks questions about their possible effects.
Choosing and Using Books in the First School by Peggy Heeks. Macmillan, 1981. A thorough guide to the selection and use of books, including useful annotated book lists.
The Design of Learning Spaces by Peter Smith. Council for Educational Technology, 1974. Well-illustrated report of one year pilot

research project.

Dewey Decimal Classification for British Schools compiled by Mary South. A wholly new edition, available from Don Gresswell.

A First Computer Dictionary by Brian Samways and Tony Byrne-Jones. Macmillan, 1984. A simple and useful introduction for people meeting computers for the first time.

The New Media Challenge by H Trowbridge. Macmillan Educational, 1974. Not so 'new' now but well worth considering.

Non-Book Media in Junior Schools: a handbook of practical advice by Peter James. School Library Association, 1977. A guide based on personal experience. Complementary to this book.

Open School, Open Society by H A Pluckrose. Evans Bros, 1975. Written by a headmaster who really practises what he preaches. Out of print but copies may be available at local centres.

Surrounded by Books by R W Purton. Ward Lock, 1970. Also out of print but still a very sound, readable and sensible book.

The Way Ahead: the organization and staffing of libraries and learning resources in schools in the 1980s. School Library Association, 1980. A policy statement. Three appendices are useful guides to the selection, coordination and maintenance of hardware and software.

Scottish Council for Educational Technology
A Resource Centre is a State of Mind
The Setting Up of a Resource Centre, 1) Basic ideas 2) Planning and staffing 3) Retrieval systems.
The first publication is of special help to those just starting on the idea of having a resource centre.

School Librarian
This is a quarterly magazine free to all members of the School Library Association. It contains practical professional articles and comments. The book reviews (arranged in age groups) are numerous and evaluative. Occasional reviews of information technology.

Times Educational Supplement
Special supplements on children's books. Reviews by experts. Weekly edition regularly contains interesting and informative reviews of software very pertinent in the school context.

Index

Pages which include illustrations are indicated by '*ill*'; pages in the bibliography are shown as '*bib*'. Where there are two or more references for a topic, any major reference is shown in **bold**.

143